This book is dedicated to the creators and participants of the world-wide Goth scene.

ACKNOWLEDGMENTS

Thanks are offered to all those individuals who provided personal experiences and factual information via interviews and correspondence during the trying period of the pandemic lockdowns and social distancing. Special appreciation is owed to Myke Hideous, Marty "Mr. Haunt" Coleman, the Countess for proofreading the manuscript and offering suggestions on content and style, and to Carlo Pisapia whose idea it was to undertake the writing of this book. Finally, special gratitude needs be extended to my three adult children—Lauren, Johnny, and Dan—for inspiring and reinforcing my interest and assimilation into the alternative music scene, notwithstanding the embarrassment it frequently caused them.

PREFACE

The subject of this book is the Goth-industrial scene centered primarily around New York City from its heyday in 1990 to its COVID-driven pause in 2020. It is not about *Gothic music*, or *Goth rock* as it is sometimes called. It is not about the much larger *dance-club nightlife* scene in NYC. It takes in what the author deems to be the broad historical and cultural milieu that nourished a specific social and aesthetic group of people: the Goths of Greater NYC and the institutions that served them—their roots, their common interests, their shared experience, and their uniqueness as a subculture. For many, even most, scenesters, the terms *Goth* and *postpunk* are used interchangeably, even in this book, although this is intrinsically problematic. In musical parlance, Goth refers to a *style*, whereas *post-punk* refers to a certain *era*: the 1980s. This was a period of time when punk had yielded its singularity, giving rise to a richly diverse yet recognizably integrated musical style. The trappings of punk—the disheveled hair, the mohawks, the iconoclastic appearance, and anarchistic outlook of punk—distinguished the new artists in that era that discarded the conventions and entertainment industry standards. MTV videos showcased them in their ragged splendor.

Years of participating in and reading and writing about the subculture that is the subject of this book have led me to the conclusion that, regardless of semantic issues, the terms *Goth* and *postpunk* are generally used as synonyms by the majority of speakers and writers.

The sequence of this book is not strictly chronological. But the reader cannot help noticing that, while older Goths and nostalgia buffs deem the eighties and early nineties to have been the "golden age of Goth," the highest levels of expression of this postpunk subculture occurred during the period of the 2000s and 2010s. The Covid lockdowns interrupted this phenomenon at its peak. There was seemingly endless delay in the reopening of Goth venues as well as eventual relocation of most of these to Brooklyn, and I found I could no longer pursue the lifestyle in person. I had perhaps aged out of the scene. Much may have happened in the reawakening after Covid lockdowns, but that is not the subject of this book.

INTRODUCTION

This book does not attempt to serve as a compendium for all things Goth. For that, the readers are referred to Andi Harriman's thorough history of Goth in her book *Some Wear Leather Some Wear Lace: The Worldwide Compendium of Postpunk and Goth in the 1980s* and to numerous previous works by journalists Mick Mercer and Gaven Baddeley.

Instead, this book traces an intimate journey of one person from the everyday world and outlook of a divorced, middle-aged, middle-class physician and mature family man into the netherworld of countercultural events and social life of the Goth music scene, referred to herein as the New Dark Age. The idea behind it is to report only those elements of the scene that the author personally experienced. There is no claim of completeness on the subject of Goth, or the New Dark Age for that matter. Only the experiences and insights that were acquired firsthand are reported.

What this book does attempt is to give the reader a sense of the breadth and interrelated diversity of the sources and various tributaries that feed the Goth scene placed in a personal historical context. Profiles of some exemplary personalities, famous or not, whose stories help elucidate the subjective experience are included. Sincere apologies are offered to those participants and creators of the Goth scene who are not profiled. Time and space considerations made it impossible to include all those who deserved mention.

It is hoped that those who participated in the scene will concur in recognizing the ideas and events described herein and that those who remain outside the scene will find empathy, interest, and enlightenment about this peculiar cultural phenomenon.

Facts reported on the history of the Goth-industrial scene are not claimed to be authoritative or minutely accurate but rather reflect the perceptions and recollections of the author.

HOW I BECAME INVOLVED IN THE GOTH SCENE

One evening, in late spring of 1990, I was invited to the birthday party of a friend, well-known artist and actor Federico, at a tavern in Garfield, New Jersey. Federico was a stellar graduate of the School of Visual Arts, a New York institution with a national reputation, and a prominent figure in the Italian American community of Paterson, New Jersey. I knew him because I frequented his neighborhood to attend the charming coffee shop and emporium San Remo on Twenty-First Avenue in what was historically called the People's Park section of Paterson.

His work was featured in an annual compendium of young, up-and-coming artists: *Illustrators Annual.* I had been a serious amateur artist all my life, both pre- and postdivorce. This was the peculiar consequence of my very early life. My father, a printer, made it a practice to bring home stacks of paper from the shop, bestowed on me so that I could amuse myself by drawing as early as age two or three. This practice continued my entire childhood and adolescence. Even in my darkest hours of my failing marriage, I managed to create a portfolio of drawings, pastels, watercolor, and acrylic paintings without training of any sort. Federico had looked at my paintings and professed to be impressed. He even accompanied me on shopping trips to find frames suitable for what he considered to be genuinely accomplished works of art. He praised my works without even a hint of lording his superior training over my efforts. In that regard, I found Federico to be affable, self-confident, and an artist I could collaborate with and perhaps learn from. I took the opportunity to observe him at work at his easel. I admired Federico's professional-level skills and had cultivated a friendship between us largely on that basis.

From time to time, and with increasing frequency, I would pal along with Federico on forays into NYC where he had contacts in the arts and avant-garde community. He introduced me to galleries, clubs, cafes, and not least of all, interesting people. This was a world I was desperate to sample, having been frustrated in my efforts to explore it during the two decades of medical training and practice-building in which I had been engaged since medical school.

In addition, at the time, I was navigating the breakup of my marriage of twenty-two years. In the last several years of the deteriorating relationship, I had sought solace in renewed efforts at expressing myself through art. Having devoted virtually all my attention outside my medical professional activities to my marriage and my adolescent children, I now found that all of the person, and the values, that had been me had dissolved or evaporated. Like it or not, I was forced to consider means by which to reinvent myself. I was open to those elements and forces that now seemed to surround me in my new situation. It was like immersion in a strange new land. I had to learn the language in order to survive and thrive. Simultaneous and parallel to this, the culture in which I had grown up—the traditional values, Sunday dinner, the shining city on the hill, codes of behavior, the traditions of the past, the values upheld by society, the familiar mode of dress, the standards of popular music—also seemed to be undergoing a metamorphosis.

I had dabbled in various forms: drawing, sculpting, carving, and painting. Working in acrylics on canvas in the basement of the marital home, I had executed a series of starkly realistic still-life artworks that reflected my claustrophobic yet focused vision from the cellar to which I had exiled myself—as background rough brick walls; a battered flea-market clarinet; a miniature bust of J. S. Bach that should have sat upon a piano, instead surrounded by raw lumber under a galvanized electrical junction box; an old-fashioned flash camera; a stuffed crow; an antique clock-radio.

I attended Federico's birthday celebration, hosted by his girlfriend at the time, Jackie. The event was held in the back family room of the tavern where there were several picnic tables and benches and a long table on which the buffet was laid out. One or two guests greeted me and chatted a bit before returning to their circle of friends, asking the usual get-acquainted questions regarding how one came to know the honoree of the party. There wasn't much else in the way of interaction between me and the other guests. I could not help but feel somewhat distant and removed from the young blue-collar crowd.

Around 10:00 p.m., I figured to say my goodbyes and head back to my unhappy marital home. But Federico called me back before I could leave, asking me to stay for coffee and pastries. I cheerfully agreed to stay. After getting my coffee and pastry at the buffet, I returned to my seat at the otherwise empty table. Other guests rose, served themselves, and returned to the original groupings of two, three, or four at their respective tables. It was getting late, and I had consumed my dessert and was about to leave when a young woman entered the room and began greeting the guests already there. I thought it odd that a guest would arrive for a party at 11:00 p.m., which was an hour well past when I would normally be at home.

She was petite, pretty, and dark-haired—in fact, a sister of Jackie, the party's hostess. She was coiffed with a Cleopatra-style hairdo and wore exotic, generous mascara, which added to the Egyptian look. She was breathtakingly beautiful. Now I felt myself to be even further distant from the composition of the crowd. She wore a black leather bikini top, below which her midriff was bare. Formfitting black tights and bulky ankle-high black boots completed what seemed to me a jarringly incongruous outfit. In the middle-class, professional circles in which I moved, an individual so attired would be looked upon with suspicion, even derision. But the exotic perfection of her appearance, her Hollywood-high cheekbones, and chiseled features overruled any objection one might have.

I had no context in which to place the look she was sporting. It wasn't a typical, true Egyptian outfit. It was something else. Was it, I wondered, within the conventions of some avant-garde postmodern subculture? One of the reasons I had cultivated the association with Federico was to be exposed to the avant-garde, particularly that associated with New York City. I had for decades been assiduously detached from any and all manifestations of the nearby metropolis—hub of arts, entertainment, and bohemian culture. This had been due to constraints arising from my profession and the long, unhappy marriage from which I was in the process of being liberated.

Like anyone who grew up in Jersey City, in my teen years, I had made forays into Greenwich Village (had attended beat poetry readings, pubs, and even a jazz club), but my adult obligations and professional and middle-class involvements had put an end to all that, pushing it decades into the past. Perhaps with access to this new, dark world, I would satisfy unfulfilled interests I had once had in the beatnik/bohemian world of the 1960s as I had imagined them as an adolescent.

As the party continued, under the pretense of getting up and sitting back down with refills of coffee, I found myself changing my place, each time seating myself closer to the fascinating, alluringly costumed, beautiful young woman. I was amazed at how little I understood of the conversation that I overheard between the beautiful creature and those with whom she chose to be seated. Although I couldn't follow the conversation, I was fixated on the husky contralto voice of this bewitching enchantress. I caught fragments of a conversation. The names that came up—music clubs both here in New Jersey and across the river in New York—were completely unfamiliar. So were the names of musicians, bands, and events. None of it was anything that should have aroused or attracted my interest. The charismatic presence of the Cleopatra-coiffed woman allowed me to dismiss any reservations or hesitation I might harbor against eavesdropping.

With the next coffee refill, I moved to the table where she was seated, but apart from being asked to introduce myself and learn the names of those seated around me, I engaged in little other conversation. I continued to act like spectator. Eventually, the party drew to a close, and guests bid each other adieu. I stayed back as one by one, or in pairs, the guests exited from the room.

As the enchanting woman was making her way to the door, she turned to bid me good night, reached into her purse for a personal business card that she then handed to me with a smile but no further explanation. Taking it, I thanked her and watched her leave. I glanced at the card that had a phone number but no address; and in the center, in elegant art deco script, was the name "Carmela," similar to that of the feminine vampire from Le Fanu's gothic novel. Oddly, it was also my mother's original name at baptism; but she had changed it, as it was too foreign sounding, to the Americanized "Milly." Above the name "Carmela," in smaller typeface line, was "Fashion faces by." In one corner was the title "Hair Design." I pondered and eventually concluded that she was both a makeup artist and a hairdresser. The phone number was a local private number. I stayed staring at it for some time after she had gone, determined to find a way to see this beguiling person again.

When I mentioned my fascination for Jackie's sister to my friend Federico several days later, he was amused, noting that she was just twenty-two years old. I was somewhat chagrined to realize that twenty-two was exactly half my age, forty-four. She was interested in art, he told me. Perhaps, he suggested, I might find it fun and interesting to give her instructions in painting. I was thunderstruck by that idea. What could possibly be as joyful and thrilling as spending time teaching and sharing my experience and thoughts about art with a charmingly eager and accepting young, aspiring artist? I thought I must take steps to put this appealing plan into effect!

Within the next few days, I spent an inordinate amount of time inspecting my hair situation in the mirror to ascertain the earliest moment when I could justify calling for a haircut. I decided, perhaps a week or two prematurely, to wait no longer and place the call.

Carmela answered, speaking in that same charming, husky contralto. She asked if I preferred to have my haircut at the salon where she worked or at her home. I was jubilant to accept her offer to provide my haircut at her home the next day.

She was waiting by the wrought-iron gate in front of her house when I arrived, not so glamorously decked out as at the party but still graceful and stunning in a T-shirt and black tights. She greeted me warmly, in a manner that reflected her ancestral Sicilian hospitality that was automatically extended to a "friend of a friend," in this case, Federico. She led me to her apartment on the second floor and bid me to seat myself on a couch while she completed a haircut that she had started on a young man now wrapped in a plastic tablecloth occupying a stool in her kitchen.

No sooner did I sink into the well-worn sofa than a cat jumped up onto the arm of the couch and began circling me. I looked up where, stretched across the ceiling, was a novelty-store, black-string, Halloween-decor spiderweb; and yet Halloween was many months away. I was seated in front of a TV, which was turned on but not tuned to any channel. Instead, it displayed a hissing, flickering, electronic snowstorm of static.

Next to the TV was a large poster that completely befuddled and, to some extent, disturbed me. The main image was of two naked females, seated on a wide rocking chair, close enough to be joined at the hips and shoulders—a bizarre sculpture of conjoined twins. Their ankles were crossed. They were bald but for simulated flames atop their identical heads. The scene was very starkly lit so that the two pair of breasts were jarringly highlighted. The image was in black and white. Scrawled above the paired, identical female figures was a distinctively handwritten logo, "Jane's Addiction." And across the bottom, in squeezed, elongated, mechanical font, was the statement, "Nothing's Shocking." I found it, well, shocking; yet I was proud of having smuggled myself into this yet-to-be-explored demimonde.

Disoriented, almost dizzy, I recall little of the conversation we held during the haircut. When it was done, I left with a promise to return the next time I needed a haircut, but wishing I could find another excuse to come back, hopefully sooner. I needed to find another reason to encounter this charismatic creature. Over the next couple of months, I returned for several haircuts, during which my fascination with Carmela deepened. Her modest, unaffected personality seemed a perfect match to her extraordinary physical beauty. I found her soft, slightly hoarse voice and effortless way of speaking to be captivating. I remembered Federico's suggestion that I might develop a relationship in which I would offer her instruction in painting, in art, in general. The idea was enchanting. I knew I was too old, too mature, to pursue a romantic relationship. I was not even drawn to that idea. I was given to fantasizing a relationship in which I would mentor her in the art of painting.

I yearned to know her better, to develop a friendship, perhaps around painting as Federico had suggested. I didn't know where to start with regards to music. I had been listening to the then-popular new-age music, experimental, ambient sounds and minimalism that I learned about on National Public radio show *New Sounds*. So, on subsequent haircut visits, I brought homemade tapes that I had prepared for her, featuring Vangelis, the progressive composer and electronic musician. I thought his album *Heaven and Hell* was most apt. It featured intense, ethereal, and macabre sounds suitable for a horror-movie soundtrack. I thought it might convince her that I fit right in with the dark culture of which she seemed to be a representative. I didn't realize that her scene was largely based upon rhythmic dance music.

I scoured record stores for music by artists like Sisters of Mercy and Jane's Addiction, hoping that these might somehow help us form a link. I guessed that she might be interested in the classic horror movies of the 1930s and '40s, which were such a significant interest of mine and which seemed a perfect fit to what I deemed to be her style. Carmela showed no signs of interest in anything that could bind us into a relationship.

But she was never far from my thoughts. When I drove past her house en route to my duties at the hospital, I hoped to see her at the wrought-iron gate where she had greeted me on that first haircut appointment. Perhaps such a staged encounter would open the door to friendly conversation that might lead to actual friendship. But such sightings never happened. I pondered in what other ways I could arrange to run into her without resorting to the reprehensible practice of stalking.

Over the next few weeks, I poured my intentions out to anyone whom I understood to be in the know. Someone suggested I look for Carmela at a dance club, the Loop Lounge, in Passaic. I began frequenting that venue, packed with a college crowd, every weekend, but without success. Still, it was the only lead with which I had come up.

On one such visit to the Loop Lounge, I ran into a young acquaintance, Giorgio, whom I knew from the Italian coffeehouse we both frequented in Paterson. He was confused and a little amused to encounter me, whom he knew only as "the doctor" from the coffee shop. He was curious as to my presence since I was obviously twenty years senior to the general population at the Loop.

"Doctor, what are you doing here?" he asked.

I told him about my interest in encountering the beautiful girl named Carmela.

"Carmela," he scoffed. "She doesn't come here. She goes to the Pipeline." He was referring to a notorious punk club deep in the decaying heart of Newark, New Jersey's squalid inner city, the car theft capital of the world. Could a person such as I venture to the Pipeline? Would I be admitted at the door? What were the codes by which denizens of the punk scene evaluated and treated outsiders like me, I wondered. But I decided then and there to follow up on his recommendation. I would go to the Pipeline if I could find someone who would show me how to get there. I turned to the young artist friend Federico whose birthday party I had just attended. He agreed to accompany me.

Under the stress of my failing marriage and removal from the marital home and the attendant anguish of separation from my children, I began to question my own identity—the person I was and had been for the past forty-four years. I sought entry into this largely unexplored subculture that Carmela seemed to represent. In my grandiose delusions, I imagined myself in the chaste role of her mentor, somewhat like that of the phantom of the opera tutoring the young soprano Christine. But in a reversal of that relationship, I was interested in having her, Carmela, lead me into the mysterious, dark subculture rather than the reverse.

THE PIPELINE

Arriving in Newark at around nine thirty, we parked our car and approached the Pipeline. A large white illuminated sign stood straight out above the entrance door. The panel on which the name or logo might be displayed was completely missing. Instead, two six-foot fluorescent light bulbs, now exposed by the absence of the title panel, flickered and buzzed into the night, announcing exactly nothing. A rusted metal drum sat in the opening of a greasy gravel-covered driveway, closed in by a tall chain-link, barbed-wire-topped fence. Burning lumber within the drum lit up the faces of two tough-looking young men who stood around it, warming themselves and puffing on cigarettes. I had to look twice to confirm what was then, to me, a novel observation. One of the men had evidence of a tattoo in a place I had never before seen, his neck. Thick, blue-black, and abstract in its design, the tattoo snaked up above his collar and into the soft jugular notch below his Adam's apple. They didn't speak to us, and we didn't speak to them.

Entering the Pipeline, we found the place practically empty. The floor was bare wood. There was a bar on the left. A bartender was setting up his station and wiping the glass refrigerator case behind him with a dirty rag. There were several stools riveted to the floor, but at least one of them was missing a rivet or two, such that it made it hazardous to sit upon it except with the utmost care.

"Where was everybody?" I asked myself.

Responding to my befuddled expression, the bartender spoke up. "Most of the crowd doesn't show up until eleven o'clock or midnight."

I should have guessed. We elected not to sit or order a drink but to walk straight through the bar into the dark room in back, the dance hall. Dark it was, with a squeaky rotating light, intermittently throwing faint cones of red, yellow, and blue into the darkness. A statuesque beauty with a perfectly straight-up black mohawk and wearing a white men's T-shirt, short shorts, and ankle-high boots was dancing a kind of modern, free-form, but energetic dance to the high-decibel music coming from the huge multiple speakers in the corners of the room. The dancer moved to the overpowering and compelling rhythm of what sounded like the remorseless machinery of a World War II-era weapons factory. I understood how it drove her to the kinetic gyrations she was performing. Over and above the pounding rhythmic percussion, there were voluminous synthetic strings pouring a luscious melody with voices—high, mournful, and agitated—that seemed to speak of some terrible crime or horrific hallucination.

I loved it. I was now on a quest to find the source of that music. I looked toward a lighted corner of the room where a plywood DJ's booth stood, high above and looking down upon the dance floor. The DJ wore a bandana, heavy false eyelashes, bright-red lipstick, and a five o'clock shadow. I stood on the first step up the ladder leading to the booth and asked him what was playing.

"Skinny Puppy," was the reply.

Another enigma. What the hell kind of answer was that? I wanted to know the name of the artist or band. What did "Skinny Puppy" mean? I stepped down from the DJ's booth.

After a while, and feeling weird about being the only people in attendance at this bizarre location, we left. We drove off in silence, because it took some time for the ringing in our ears to quit such that we could begin a conversation. Federico explained to me that Skinny Puppy was the name of a famous industrial, he called it, band.

Now I had another powerful motive, besides scouting for Carmela, to visit the Pipeline where I would hear the music of Skinny Puppy. I got up the courage to start driving to Newark every Saturday night, immersing myself in the strange but engrossing music—industrial or otherwise—to which the punkish crowd danced at the Pipeline.

In order to learn what I was listening to, I befriended the Saturday-night DJ, Bobby Lisi, who operated a record store in Montclair, a hip middle-class community located halfway between my home and Newark's Pipeline club. He served as a source of general as well as insider information on the latest music scene, sharing his knowledge while building an enthusiastic customer base. The record store was called Café Soundz, and it was attached to a clothing/accessories and collectibles boutique, Two Tone. The latter name referred to the predominant color scheme that everyone at the Pipeline wore, namely, black with, at most, only an occasional touch of white, shunning the whole spectrum of hues of attire. He invited me into the DJ's booth where I watched him select and queue up the series of songs that he played, sometimes off vinyl records, others in the newly popular, compact disc format.

During the months that followed, I became quite the expert on what was current in what was then termed the alternative music

scene, hoping that this would somehow improve my standing with the sought-after Carmela, should I run into her and try to maintain a conversation. But I had no luck at this venue, although I continued to go there every Saturday night with one friend or another, depending upon who was available.

Not everything in the repertoire being played was of the industrial category, although there certainly was an abundance of Nine Inch Nails, KMFDM, and Ministry. Both obvious and subtle differences distinguish industrial music from Goth, but the fact is that for some fans, they both converge upon the same specific taste in music. All of the lineup was however ultimately rhythmic, danceable, and heavily reliant on electronic instrumentation and enhancement. The themes were often harsh, defiant, and aggressive. The wantonly dancing patrons were expressing and sublimating their own anger and personal frustrations through the alter ego of the angry, lost, and disconsolate industrial musicians.

As I groped for some level of understanding or familiarity, I thought of industrial music as having roots in new-age electronica, in which I had been briefly interested through listening to late-night public radio broadcasts. Back in the 1970s, I had been somewhat fascinated by seminal artists like the German electronic project Tangerine Dream and, later, Kraftwerk, to which I became exposed via MTV and on a free-form radio station WFMU, then out of Upsala College. The difference was that the industrial, electronica heard at the Pipeline took a dark, aggressive turn into the realm of anger, discontent, and protest of the world as it is. It coordinated with the unhappy predicament in which I found myself during the transitional years as I went from an unhappy marriage into a solitary life and a socioeconomic quagmire that yearned for a voice. Because of this personal connection, I found the brutal, pounding, and complex beats; the mysterious lyrics; and innovative production style to be exhilarating.

I wasn't totally naïve of nightlife and avant-garde culture. As my divorce went through, I had become a reader of the *Village Voice*, the well-known NYC tabloid read by the hip and alternative communities. It was in the *Voice* that clubs and theaters of the off-off-triple-off Broadway-type-made announcements. Poetry readings and open-microphone amateur performances were announced here. Even some punk bands and singer-songwriters had ads, and I began visiting some of these joints once I was out on my own. I was still shy going to places like CBGBs, of which I had heard warnings, or other places that I had never heard of at all. For the time, I was preparing to take another step in the direction of the Pipeline—and the elusive Carmela.

A completely unrelated event, a brush with a deadly disease, was to forge a link between the Goth-industrial world and me.

RABIES

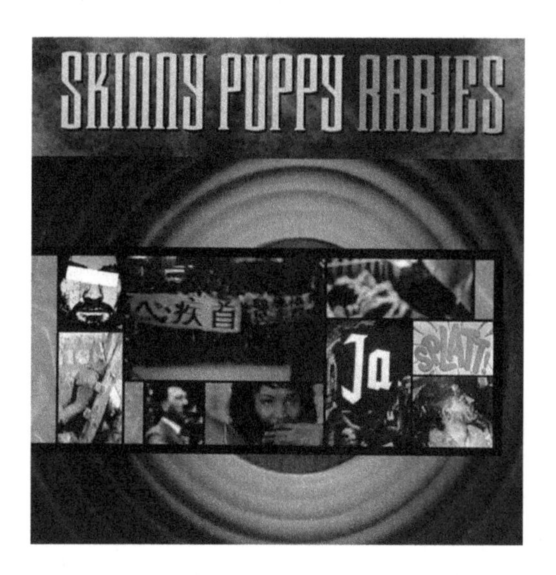

One afternoon, during the weeks that followed my marital separation, I was invited to a backyard barbecue at the suburban home of an aunt and uncle in Mountainside, New Jersey. Their yard was situated adjacent to the sprawling Echo Lake Park, with no fence or barriers intervening. As we went about consuming our meal and engaging in family chatter, a scrawny black cat wandered into the yard and began circling the table. My aunt expressed displeasure at the cat's presence, stating that this was a feral beast that inhabited the wooded area of the nearby park. Without giving it real thought, I didn't find any of that objectionable.

I had acquired, at home, a sweet, friendly black cat, Hjalmar, named after the villain portrayed by Boris Karloff in the 1935 motion picture *The Black Cat.* My Hjalmar was friendly and dignified, with a superficial resemblance to this unwelcome backyard intruder. Impulsively, I took a slice of salami and reached down to cozy up to the cat with a friendly offering. In an instant, the beast lashed out with a paw, its claws bared, and ripped the slice of salami from my fingers, slashing my hand slightly but sufficiently deeply to draw blood. I cursed the creature and returned to my meal, dabbing with a napkin at my wounded hand. When my aunt noticed my injury, she expressed not just routine concern but some actual alarm.

"That cat is dangerous," she said. "It lives in the woods around raccoons and bats. Just the other day, the cops came around and had to shoot some raccoons because they had *rabies.*"

Rabies! What a thought. The most horrible way to die for man or beast. A fatal brain disease that crept up the nerves from where one got bitten, causing unbearable agitation and, worst of all, agonizingly painful convulsions of the pharynx, rendering the victim unable to drink or consume anything due to the throat seizures it provokes. Even saliva trickling in the back of the throat could set this off, so the victim, rather than swallowing, drools or foams the mouth. It was just too hideous to contemplate. Bats and raccoons are common carriers. It usually results from a bite. But, I thought, the cat may have licked its paw, planting the virus on its claws before deeply scratching me.

I immediately lost interest in the meal. After placing some useless calls to the local emergency room, I decided it was best to call Animal Control. They responded quickly, and within half an hour, there was a van at my aunt's address. Unable to catch the cat on the spot, the animal control officer placed a trap and took my personal information. I washed my hand and applied an ointment, sardonically imagining that these were but feeble measures to take against this potentially horrible malady.

The weekend passed, and then I began to come down with strange physical symptoms. I had chills and malaise. A lymph node began to swell in my armpit on the same side as the scratch. My hand wound healed rapidly, forming a strong, dry scab. Several days into the following week, I received a phone call from the Board of Health advising me that the cat had died. They were sending the cat's brain for examination to Trenton to be tested for rabies. It would be several more days before we would know the results. In a state or alarm, I headed to the emergency room of my local hospital.

I explained my situation to the emergency room physician. She opened her manual and read off the recommended treatment. We both learned that it was essential that treatment with rabies vaccine be initiated on the first, or at latest, the second day. But that opportunity was now half a week in the past. The wound should have been injected with rabies immune globulin while it was still open. But my wound was completely sealed over by then. Rabies vaccine should have been administered on day one or two, then repeated at three days, six days, two weeks, four weeks, and three months. I was already way behind on hoping to prevent or treat this vile death sentence. The emergency room physician decided to try to catch up, jamming the first three vaccine injections into this one visit: one in the shoulder above the wounded hand and one into each buttock. They left me feeling like a cannonball had been implanted in each injection site, but they were my only hope, so I thought. I remained ill the rest of the week. Three days later, I went back to the emergency room and received another pair of buttock injections that, like the first set, left me barely able to walk.

Friday, the word came that the lab in Trenton had completed the tests. The cat did not have rabies! I felt overwhelmingly relieved. The fever—alarming, but a mere coincidence—subsided, and I felt the need to get out and enjoy life with renewed enthusiasm. I summoned my teenage son John to come with his friend on a Saturday visit to New York City, where we could see sights and perhaps take in a movie at an art cinema house. The two boys and I went to the Film

Forum, where there was a summer screen festival featuring classic, old black-and-white sci-fi, fantasy, and horror movies.

Afterward, we strolled around the Village gawking at sights and browsing shops. One of these was a record store. While the boys riffled through both vinyl and CD format albums by their favorite bands, a thought came to me. This was the Village! This was New York! Maybe it was here that I could find a record by...what was it? Skinny Puppy! I approached a salesclerk, hesitatingly inquiring if there was something like an *industrial* music section.

"What are you looking for?" he asked, seeing the need to direct my search.

"Skinny, er, Puppy," I replied hesitantly as if I might be laughed at for the absurdity of my response.

"That's in the rock section," he replied. "Alphabetically." I headed to the "Rock" rack and looked in the alphabetical *S* section. There it was! Packaged in one of those foot-long, flattened cardboard envelopes in which CDs came in those days, here was the goal of my search. Standing out in bright-orange lettering from the black-and-gray background were the words, in a weird font, "Skinny Puppy" in all capital letters. Below it, by way of unexpected coincidence, was the title of the album: *Rabies*. I hurried to the cashier, made my purchase, and eagerly anticipated returning home for my first listen.

It is difficult to describe the effect that the *Rabies* album had on me. Living alone in my second-floor walk-up bachelor pad, I spent much of my waking hours listening to it, whether I was painting or just sitting with the liner notes trying to fathom the enigmatic lyrics. Each song on the album had a unique and, for me, unprecedented flair. Most were intensely rhythmic, only somewhat musical. There were cadenzas of electronic gadgetry; hoarse, plaintive vocals; and frequent intrusions by sound clips (samples, they're called) from movies, radio shows, television, and political speeches, even from other commercial recordings. These samples often produced an eerie effect of weird juxtaposition. I deemed the work to be somewhere in the strange realm between patterned noise and actual music.

I was intrigued by the perplexing lyrics over which I poured incessantly. It isn't uncommon for song lyrics or poetry to ignore the rules of grammar and syntax, but these went a step further. I hypothesized that the lyricist had sat with a dictionary and picked words and phrases, not to express coherent ideas but rather by their overwhelmingly negative and mood-lowering connotations. I was particularly fascinated by the words to Skinny Puppy's masterpiece "Warlock," which I read and reread countless times trying to find the story it attempted to tell. Terms like *ritual and resister*, *dog's body*, and *comatose* are sprinkled meaningfully into the libretto but without conducing to an orderly, comprehensible narrative of any sort.

Although every track on that album is uniquely fantastic, artistic, and original, there was one track that stood out even higher: "Worlock." Typical of Skinny Puppy likes to play with words, syntax, and spelling in the titles and their works. Thus, sometimes it's spelled "Warlock," sometime "Worlock." The discrepancy is just part of a punk rock disregard for rules of spelling. "Worlock," or "Warlock," however you choose to spell it, has an unusual and compelling rhythmic beat. It starts with layers of menacing electronic drones, then bursts into the most mechanical, jittery, repetitive rhythm that can be imagined, over which the vocalist, Nivek Ogre, growls or screams these disconsolate lyrics in a clear and articulate manner. It retains an ongoing sense of crescendo throughout, eventually leading up to an actual and even more frantic crescendo. I began to look on this piece of music as standing alongside the greatest and most singular works of music. Beethoven's Fifth comes to mind. Another candidate would be Also Sprach Zarathustra by Richard Strauss. Nietzsche had offered the lyric opera *Carmen* as holding such a place. I imagined "Warlock" with the same status.

After *Rabies* I went in pursuit of every other album or EP they had ever produced. I realized that I was coming late to the game. Here I was, an utter novice in the very infancy of my Skinny Puppy fandom, yet the band itself was conceivably already past its prime. Skinny Puppy had formed in 1982, exactly a decade before my happenstance discovery. They had already put out their masterpiece album *Too Dark Park* and were about to release what was supposed to be their final album, entitled *Last Rights*, which I purchased on the day it reached the stores.

Consulting rock-music periodicals over the next few years, I learned to revere vocalist Nivek Ogre and cEvin Key; but I also recognized the complex and indispensible roles played by Dwayne Goettel, the classically trained keyboardist who was responsible for those eerily appropriate sound samples, and Austrian-born synth-bassist Bill Leeb. Skinny Puppy came to occupy such a central and monumental role in my life and *Weltanschauung* that I began to experience concern, if not actual anxiety, that they might at some future date retire and be taken away from me. Terror struck me when Ogre quit the band in 1995 and, worse still, Goettel died of the "traditional" heroin overdose. Despondent, I sought consolation in hoping that I could acquire a similar, but clearly improbable, fanaticism for Bill Leeb's spin-off industrial project called Front Line Assembly. Fortunately, Ogre's absence from the band was brief, and I was soon able to continue collecting and listening to new works by them, including *Process*, *Greater Wrong*, *Myth Maker*, and *Weapon*.

Although each broke new ground, the newer works continued to uphold the high standards of creativity and signature style of the earliest works *Bites*, *Mind*, and *Vivisect VI*. Only one album fell short of my expectations: the 2011 *Handover*, which produced several tracks that might have served to induce sleep rather than the sought-for agitation that Skinny Puppy usually served up. When I posted a review of *Handover* on a Skinny Puppy Facebook page, I received abundant hate mail but, fortunately, no death threats.

In my mind, a mystique became attached to Skinny Puppy and the entire category of industrial music. I wondered if its rise signaled some kind of new, dark age. It seemed plausible, namely, that our civilization and the entire world might be entering into an era of cultural decline like the Dark Ages of European history. If so, I saw myself as beginning to meet the challenge of successfully navigating this New Dark Age while struggling to hold onto my core values and beliefs. Because of estrangement from my marriage, I was prepared to throw off much of my former self, but hopefully not my original bedrock identity. What I really needed was a virtual label to which to attach myself, some way of expressing myself, as I've been compelled to do all my life, but in terms that were drawn from this sea change that was taking place in the darkening world. I called it the New Dark Age.

A HEART TRANSPLANT TO THE LOWER EAST SIDE: THE BANK

Like many teenagers, my older son, Johnny, and his friends were deeply involved in rock music, at a level that some would term fanatical and others, scholarly. Their favorite band, Rush, traverses the broad zone that runs between progressive rock and heavy metal. Thus, they were on the alert for metal bands that might be performing live shows in the area, of which they could be proud as neighbors. So it came to pass that they got wind that a heavy Goth metal band known as the Empire Hideous was scheduled to perform at a nightclub in Manhattan. I harbored a twenty-some years pent-up desire to reexplore the alternative cultural scene that I remembered with such fondness from long-past visits to Greenwich Village in my late adolescence. But the boys were wary of traveling both to and within the city, so I agreed to provide transportation and accompany them. I wondered if by doing so, I might chance upon Carmela.

The show was to be held at a performance space/nightclub called the Bank, situated at the corner of First Avenue and East Houston. It was the early nineties, before the Giuliani cleanup of the town; and the streets of NYC were still, by legend, at least, held to be somewhat dangerous. That didn't really matter except to make the trip we would make seem to us more adventurous. The Bank was a nightclub that had taken over a stately edifice of an actual former bank and, in the interim, had once been the studio of abstract expressionist artist Jaspar Johns.

The details of the lead-up to the show were not worthy of remembering. What happened there is of greater importance. I recall the podium, the entrance doorway, and the gargantuan bouncers standing back in support of the ticket taker or cashier. This seemed normal from my bourgeois, suburban experience. What was new was the cashier's casually clasping the hand that I had extended to pay her so she could place an ink stamp on the underside of my wrist. What we saw when we entered was curious rather than disconcerting.

The Bank, with a high-ceilinged atrium, had balconies and a bar wrapped partway around at the second level. The patrons outside and those streaming in seemed to all seemed to be wearing black, many with dyed black hair; thick, black eyeliner; sculptured eyebrows; and deep-purple or maroon lipstick—all of which stood out from their pasty-white face makeup. I thought it was tremendous fun to hang around these women styled and groomed like Carmela, who had initiated this quest. I immediately began scanning the place for her.

People were either dancing to music coming from great speakers, standing by the bars, or meandering across the floor. There were one or two groups of three or four, but widespread signs of gregariousness were absent. Most patrons stood alone, either holding a drink in hand or rocking rhythmically in place. And best of all, the women, whom I found so attractive, wore outfits that ranged from the relatively conservative look Carmela had worn at the birthday party to the full-on vampiric look of a horror-movie actress.

I had arrived at my nirvana, and I had an immediate sense of identification with these people, the Goths of NYC. I would learn the ways of this culture and find out how to fit into it. I knew there would be a group identity and shared ideas about what distinguished "creeps" from bona fide members of the scene. I knew to remain low key, observant, and to stay *sotto voce.*

At first, I didn't speak to anyone, but I perked my ears up to those nearby. From the speakers came a richly depressing baritone, singing mournfully over a piano played at a funeral-march rhythm. I liked it! Like Skinny Puppy had been to me, this could be a new musical thread to follow. So I got up the gumption to casually ask a tall young man with a completely shaved head and a chin beard, "Who is playing?" He responded with the name of the DJ. I explained that I meant the singer, the artist, not the DJ.

"Oh, I don't know. Either Nick Cave or Leonard Cohen."

I had heard of Leonard Cohen back in the 1970s but didn't understand if or how his music fit into what was being played at the Bank. I was unfamiliar with the name Nick Cave. The distinction was immediate. Skinny Puppy was industrial. But this was Goth!

I imagined that my lifelong interest in the early movies of Boris Karloff and Bela Lugosi and other giants of that cinematic style had somehow credentialed me to enter the world of Goth. It also facilitated my immediate sense of identification with these people at the Bank. If only these dark-clad, faux villains knew that I could recite from memory the sequence of *Frankenstein*, *The Wolfman*, and *Dracula* motion pictures, then, I theorized, they'd have to accept me as one of them. I hoped that if they were to learn of my fanatical celebration of Halloween or of my self-identification as an arch libertarian, they would welcome me into this social circle.

These thoughts gave way as the bombastic roar and ultradeep croaking of an electric bass guitar suddenly interrupted them. The band had begun to play. Stepping forward was a gaunt singer—dressed in black with a wide-brim, black leather, Western-style hat—gripping a microphone and belting out echo-laden lyrics in a kind of rage, while backup guitar accompaniment splashed out a seductive melody in the style that I had previously, and mistakenly, attributed to heavy metal.

This was the group the boys had come to see and hear: the Empire Hideous. It sounded good, but I was more taken up with visuals, both those of the band onstage and in the surrounding darkly costumed attendees at the show. Not much more stood out on that evening. The band performed for about an hour. When their set ended very late, we drove home to NJ. It was then that the boys informed me that the Empire Hideous was locally based and performed from place to place in north NJ.

The experience at the Bank convinced me that I must build a personal commitment bridge to NYC, but I wasn't sure how I could accomplish that. I thought perhaps my friend, the artist Federico, could help me create that bridge. His professional artistic activities brought him into the city often. I made it my business to start accompanying him whenever possible, visiting galleries and cafes and generally bumming around the Village, Soho, and the Lower East Side.

Meanwhile, Carmela apparently had become wary of my increasingly unwelcome fascination for her. After several more visits to her kitchen/salon for haircuts, and perhaps with the advice of her friends, she stopped replying to the messages I was leaving on her answering machine. I knew I had overplayed my attempts at friendship and ceased trying to establish a social relationship.

Then one evening, totally unexpectedly, she called me. I was thrilled and perplexed when I saw her identified by the caller ID. I answered with enthusiasm, completely open to whatever she might need to speak to me about.

It turned out that she was about to attend a Halloween party and needed advice regarding the costume she was planning to wear. She intended to go as Vampirella, the comic-book character. I thought it was an absolutely splendid idea. The thought of her attired as Vampirella sent my imagination soaring and filled me with delight. For some obscure reason, she assumed that I would be an authoritative source of information about the costume. Paradoxically, I was! I had in fact a collection of graphic novels and adult comic books that included a generous stack of *Vampirella* comics.

"What does Vampirella wear?" Carmela asked.

I began thumbing through the stack.

"Well, she wears a red one-piece bathing suit with a white collar and a deep plunging neckline, down to her belly button, and ankle boots. She wears ankle boots—black leather, stiletto-heel ankle boots. Long gloves too. Elbow length or sometimes shoulder length."

She thanked me and was about to hang up, when I was compelled to ask, "Where and how are you going to get those items?"

"No problem," she replied. "I think I already have all of them."

As we said goodbye and hung up, I was happy to have been chosen to render such information, but chagrined that I was not going to see her in person and certainly not invited to accompany her to the party she was about to attend. Ultimately, I took solace in having formed, from this exchange, an undefined friendly bond that went beyond haircuts. At the same time, I realized that despite our unexpected ability to connect on the basis of our both being fans of the horror comic character Vampirella, this did nothing to promote me into her social circle. I would have to find my own way into this scene.

THE YAFFA CAFÉ

A major incentive to cultivate Federico's friendship was that it gave me opportunity to satisfy my ardent desire for exposure to avant-garde culture and society, which meant hanging out with interesting people.

One of our hangouts was Café Roma, a coffeehouse and wine bar in Hoboken, the mile-square, ethnically diverse town resembling Greenwich Village on the New Jersey side of the Hudson. For me, the real attraction was Bernadette, a cute Irish waitress at the café. She was barely old enough to legally serve drinks, but I had a slight crush on her. She was way too young for me to take the flirtation as anything more than a joke. But it was fun. She was always over-the-top cheerful and smiling, although I never saw or heard her laugh. I think myself to be somewhat witty, and I usually manage to get a laugh out of girls with my dry humor. Not Bernadette. The funniest comments I could muster only evoked a blank, blinking smile suggesting that Bernadette didn't *get* it. She would just continue smiling broadly at what I thought should be sidesplitting funny. I found it endearing but also troubling and wrote it off as a sign of her immaturity. At my invitation, Federico frequently visited Café Roma with me and became familiar with the staff, including Bernadette.

One day Federico and I attended a late-night party at an apartment in the Kip's Bay section in Manhattan. He had become friends with a circle of Russian émigré artists and photographers. Someone in that circle had mentioned that an Israeli couple was planning to establish an all-night, East Village café and restaurant on Saint Marks Place, between First Avenue and Avenue A. This is the exact block that was immortalized twice: the album cover of Led Zeppelin's *Physical Graffiti* shows a row of tenements at that exact location and the site appears in a Rolling Stones video, "Waiting for a Friend." Days later, Federico received the proposal to paint a mural on an exterior front wall above the entrance to this, the Yaffa Cafe.

The mural was to be nine feet by eleven feet, starting about six feet off the ground and reaching up to around seventeen feet. It was to be based on a black-and-white photo of the wife of the owner-couple, Lika. She was portrayed in a very audacious pose. In the image, her mouth was wide open; and she wore a military officer's hat, a cowhide shawl, and rows of oversize pearls. Above and around her would be the words "Yaffa Café—Open All Night." The design had come from a photographer connected with the circle of these émigré artists.

Federico expressed doubt that he could handle this big a job single-handedly. That, I hoped, is where I would fit in. I proposed that I'd assist him by working on those parts of the painting that I could handle. It was understood that he was the professional artist, and I, the amateur. I had no idea how to go about the operation itself. But Federico knew about scaffolding and how to transfer the image from a photograph to a wall painting. He knew the kind of exterior paint to buy for a brick wall.

As far as painting, I could hold my own, but we were not on equal artistic footing. We could share painting the broader areas, but we would have to reserve the more difficult details for Federico.

Federico was unconvinced that we could pull it off. He estimated that it would take two painters a week to complete the mural. But he couldn't see how I could take on a schedule of a week spent painting while continuing my medical practice. Motivated by eagerness to participate in a real work of art, I was determined to make it happen. With enough notice, I explained that I could confine my professional obligations to one half day or the other (i.e., a morning or an afternoon). Emergencies that called me in at night wouldn't conflict with the daytime work of painting the mural.

Eventually, he became convinced and asked me to accompany him to discuss the proposed mural with the owner of the café. Mr. Ramati received us inside the Yaffa Café, which was several steps down below sidewalk level. I had no intention of speaking up. I was just tagging along to provide moral support. Mr. Ramati first proposed that we work for nothing, gratis, just to gather fame for ourselves. We rejected that! Then he proposed paying Federico $1,000 to do the job. Federico wasn't willing to settle for that, yet he eagerly wanted the job. Mr. Ramati stood firm and defended his offer. He asked rhetorically if we thought he had unlimited resources.

"What? You think I have a lot of money? I don't have money."

Then I remembered the *Illustrators Annual* publication and what it meant that Federico's work appeared in it. I spoke up.

"It's not just that the money is too little for what is basically a two-man job," I said. "Federico has a reputation to uphold. He can't let it get around that he will work for such a little amount. We couldn't take less than $2,000."

Mr. Ramati wanted to meet us halfway, at $1,500. But I rejected his offer and got him to agree to $1,800. I wasn't expecting to get paid personally, but as a friend, I wanted Federico to get the most he could.

With that settled, we set about the tasks of obtaining and constructing the scaffold and getting the brushes and paint. Federico took care of most of that himself. I joined him at the site in the early morning hours on a Monday while dawn was still hours away. Federico placed a projector on a tripod and aimed it at the wall on which the mural would be painted. He placed a photograph of what had become the familiar image of Lika, Mrs. Ramati, into the mechanism and projected it on the white wall he had painted earlier.

The scaffold he constructed had two levels. The upper level allowed me to paint the upper half of the image and reach up to the top border of the mural. The lower level gave him access to paint the lower half and the bottom margin of the mural.

The first order of business was to scurry up, armed with thick black marking crayon to trace out the basic shapes of the projected image. We marked where and how large the letters would be and outlined the details of the hat and the facial features.

The image was very stark, consisting of solid whites on a defined black background. Lika's lips, curled up into a snarl, appeared jet-black, as did the reflective vinyl bill on her officer's cap, the fabric of which was solid white in the photograph we were copying. The bib-like necklace of pearls appeared in subtler metallic shades. And then there was the cowhide shawl. While there were typical bovine spots of black and white, there was this smudged swirl, an intentional photograph artifact, distorting and flowing off the right side of the shawl like a flame. Capturing that photographic effect would be a challenge.

When the crayon tracing was done, we came down, took a break, and had breakfast. Next, armed each with brushes, we climbed up the scaffold, each with one can of black and one can of white paint. I took the upper level. I was hopeful that working initially on simple shapes like the typewriter font letters would prepare me to handle painting the hat and face. It was after all, my first and only experience with a house-painter-sized job.

The sun was up, and the projected image was no longer needed, so we shut the projector and removed it from its post on the sidewalk. Now in daylight and with the figure outlined in crayon, it was possible to lay down the basic black background around the lettering and the portrait shapes. Every application of the brush to the wall sent a tremor through the metal scaffolding, which resulted in slight wavering of the platforms underfoot. It wasn't all that disturbing, but it was noticeable and became constant. It felt sort of like standing on a small boat at a dock, requiring our cerebella to continuously adjust our balance and make ongoing adjustments in our postural musculature. Our leg and torso muscles got a prolonged workout.

I joined Federico in the early morning hours for a week, and we painted together until it was time for me to leave. Every noon, I closed my cans of paint, cleaned my brushes with turpentine, and climbed down, leaving Federico alone to continue painting. Then I dashed off to where my car was parked a few blocks away and collected the ever-present parking ticket off my windshield. Fines in those days were ridiculously cheap, $8. I'd hop into my car and speed back to New Jersey.

In half an hour (traffic also wasn't like it is today!), I was back in New Jersey at my home office where appointments were scheduled for 1:00 p.m. As I jumped out of my car, there were always several patients parked in my parking lot observing my arrival. I'd hop out and cross the lot in my paint-stained and turpentine-smelling clothes, enter my private apartment entrance door, and run up the stairs to shower and change. I cleaned up and changed fast, doing a Clark Kent routine, then descended down from my apartment to the office in a white shirt and tie, wearing a white doctor's lab coat, ready to begin my office hours on time.

We completed the painting on a Friday, and I rushed home to dress for a party at the Yaffa, celebrating the completion of the mural. Federico and I visited and hung out at the Yaffa both Saturday and

Sunday of that weekend in order to take in the praise and appreciation of patrons and passersby alike.

Federico approached me and asked if he could share with me the $1,800 remuneration he had collected from Mr. and Mrs. Ramati. I was reluctant to ask for pay because my participation had been entirely my idea, as it served my purposes as much as it did his. But on second thought, I came to the conclusion that only if I were to collect pay for the job could I consider myself at least a semiprofessional artist—and this for the first time! So I told Federico that since the total pay was $1,800, I would be happy to accept one tenth of that, $180, as compensation for my helping him with his job. He thought that was too little, but I assured him that I was satisfied. So he peeled off that amount in twenties and gave it to me with an expression of friendly appreciation.

On Sunday, leaving Federico at the Yaffa, I stopped back at the Café Roma in Hoboken for one more cappuccino and to flirt with Bernadette, the cute Irish waitress. I had some photographs I had taken during the process of painting the mural, and I wanted to show them in order to impress her. To this day, I regret having failed to take more photos to document the stages of completion of the mural. Anyhow, I went over the few pictures with Bernadette, explaining how I had finagled my way into partnering with Federico, this well-known professional artist, on a project of such magnitude and notoriety. I never felt confident that she was following my conversation, but she smiled as if she did. I mentioned that he might be stopping by but that I couldn't wait for him as I had to get home and prepare for the beginning of the coming week's medical practice obligations.

I failed, unfortunately, to debrief this cute airhead of a girl, barely out of her teens and who had a tendency to misconstrue details of conversations that I had had with her. After I left, Federico arrived, hoping to catch up with me so we could chat it up with Bernadette and friendly owner of the Hoboken café.

It didn't take long for Bernadette to inform him that I had just been there and had shown her my photos of the mural and of us engaged in the process of painting it. That's when she jumbled the narrative, stating that she understood that he, Federico, was somehow lucky to have been selected to assist me in creating this landmark piece of art. Or was it the other way around? She didn't know and surely didn't think it mattered. Did Federico help me? Or did I help Federico? To Bernadette, it was just a handful of photos.

Not however to Federico. Usually affable and easygoing, Federico's artistic and professional ego was insulted.

"Did Doktor John tell you that he painted the mural and that I was just his helper?"

Bernadette smiled, blinked, and wondered what the fuss was all about.

"I don't know. He said something like that. I don't remember exactly what he said. Whatever!"

This unfortunately ended our friendship and any hopes of ever collaborating with Federico in the future. Federico never approached me for clarification, and I never had an opportunity to refute Bernadette's misconstrual of the facts. From then on, I got the cold shoulder whenever I tried to contact him to get together. No words, harsh or otherwise, ever passed between us. I came to the understanding that he didn't want anything to do with me anymore, but I had no idea as to why. Only months or years later did I learn from a mutual acquaintance that Bernadette's confused and reversed rendering of what I told her had been sufficiently offensive for things to end up like that.

When the Ramatis asked Federico to create another mural image of Lika, similar in scale, on the back wall in the restaurant's garden, he called instead upon another young recent graduate of SVA to assist him. From that point onward, I could no longer depend upon Federico to accompany me on jaunts into NYC.

CLUBBING AT THE LOOP LOUNGE

With intentions to start frequenting the Pipeline, I acquired a motorcycle and began dressing accordingly. My entire wardrobe—apart from the collection of white shirts, ties, and suits that I wore to work as a doctor—became black: leather motorcycle jacket, black tees, black riding pants, black button-down collar shirts—and boots. I had always favored above-ankle footwear, so I shopped for boots that matched both the motorcycle outfit and the music scene. Doc Martens were all the rage, but I wanted to express a measure of individuality, so I paid a visit to Paterson's Army-Navy Surplus store for black work boots.

I kept going to the Loop Lounge to be with my friends, but I attended the Pipeline completely solo, arriving on motorcycle and wearing a motorcycle jacket, which I thought would make my presence as an outsider less conspicuous. I chose heading right into the DJ's booth as a niche by which to fit in. Bobby, the DJ and record storeowner, didn't really like my crowding him in the booth and letting people assume some arrangement existed between us. But in fact there was no arrangement. I felt it was the best place from which to get an overview of the crowd and acquire an intense learning experience by observing the business of the DJ. The booth did not, however, afford me situations in which I could make friends.

I was still more committed to the Loop Lounge where I had friends with whom I could socialize. I could take in the music as well and learn more about the scene and appreciate it. Those friends were already familiar with the Loop, as were all young eligible singles in North Jersey. Through these friends, I acquired new friends, most of whom were twenty years my junior.

My main companion to the Loop was a handsome, young pizza maker named Carmelo, and he was a perfect companion. He was extremely amiable, conversant on dozens of subjects, cultured, and open-minded. He was of Sicilian origin and had a dignified manner seen in many of his compatriots. Despite my being some fifteen years his senior, we had a great deal in common. He was abundantly sincere and sophisticated enough to relate to someone older than himself. Young women would flock to him, which I saw as a distinct benefit of cultivating his friendship.

Carmelo wasn't Goth, although he had played along with that identity during his clubbing days before I knew him. He had formal education in music and was deeply knowledgeable about all the alternative and new wave artists in whom I was interested. He was my guide, introducing me to local nightlife beyond the Loop. I soon convinced him to visit the Pipeline with me. Our life-after-dark companionship served as reinforcement of my growing interest in the Goth scene, although I still didn't have a clear idea of what *Goth* meant.

My interest in broader alternative music linked perfectly with Carmelo's almost comprehensive knowledge and appreciation of postpunk and eighties rock. He introduced me to bands like the Smiths and increased my knowledge of bands I already knew, like the Cure. In the decade previous to our friendship, he had been a fan of what was then called modern rock, which was represented mainly by British bands of the postpunk movement. For years I had dabbled in learning to speak Italian, and he helped foster that effort. Added to that was our shared interest in meeting and dating eligible women.

The music at the Loop Lounge varied quite a bit. Everyone understood it to be "alternative." Sometimes it was mechanical and electronic, called industrial. It was always danceable; and indeed, apart from the serious drinkers, the barflies, most patrons were mostly dancing most of the time. Another type of music heard there was guitar driven, the newly popular grunge sound arising from West Coast centers like Seattle.

From my teenage children, I had deepened my knowledge this new category within "alternative music." Through their influence and recommendations, I was listening to Smashing Pumpkins, Nirvana, Pearl Jam, Jane's Addiction, etc. Softer than grunge were such bands as Ned's Atomic Dustbin, R.E.M., and Jesus Jones. Then there were the girl punk bands too like L7, Bikini Kill, et al., with tattoos and nose rings to go with their new brand of music.

Carmelo closed his pizzeria at around 11:00 p.m. on Saturdays. Rather than take this as an excuse to collapse exhausted in his bed, he would usually accompany me. He would pick me up at midnight, and we'd head right over to the Loop Lounge. We would sit at the bar, socializing with a variety of characters, female and male, until the

3:00 a.m. closing time. Carmelo's circle of Loop habitués included a couple of guys with ties to the Ironbound section of Newark by virtue of their Iberian heritage: one Spanish, one Portuguese. Both were also alternative music enthusiasts. At closing, we would stretch the night out by visiting a highway diner for snacks before returning to each of our homes after 4:00 a.m.

Sunday nights, Carmelo and I would get together and visit Hoboken to hang around Café Roma. The proprietor was a pleasant and friendly young man who owned a coffeehouse in Little Italy as well as the one we attended in Hoboken. There was also the cute Irish waitress, Bernadette, too. I harbored no hard feelings toward her considering that she had ruined things between Federico and me.

My adolescent offspring had mixed responses in their attitudes toward my interest in alternative music, which they viewed as a sort of invasion. It was also terribly embarrassing that their middle-aged father was dressing, grooming, and acting like a twentysomething-year-old. It was also obvious that I was making a complete fool of myself in pursuing an after-dark lifestyle unsuited for a practicing physician. Their embarrassment at the situation was almost unbearable, as they often let me know. But at the same time, they accepted the advantages that could be gained by pandering to my relaxed standards of behavior.

On one occasion, I was persuaded to take the leap and accompany my sixteen-year-old son and his girlfriend to CBGBs to see some local punk and garage bands. I don't usually drink alcohol, but it was almost mandatory to have a bottle of beer standing on the table at which one was seated at the club, so I bought a bottle and abandoned it after one or two sips. When we drove home, our vehicle was stopped in a DWI trap. There was no way to avoid the anxiety of the situation as I tremulously handed over my license and registration papers to a cop, who scrutinized my face and shone a flashlight into my eyes to assess my state of sobriety. He determined easily enough that I was completely sober and returned my documents with the routine advice to continue driving safely.

As we drove off, and laughed the laugh of relief, I took the greatest pleasure in assessing the experience to have been my first and only encounter with the law since becoming a physician. I had also overcome my wariness about entering CBGBs, the storied Mecca of punk culture. I also took it to be a sort of baptism into my new shady late-night entertainment lifestyle.

Acrylic On Canvas 2008

LOLLAPALOOZA

In 1991, an announcement got around that there was a spectacular touring festival called Lollapalooza that was coming to New Jersey. Everybody in their twenties and thirties was planning on going to it. Against their better judgment, my teenage kids had reinforced my interest in the budding alternative music scene. Besides helping me develop knowledge and deep enthusiasm for the grunge rockers Pearl Jam, Nirvana, and Smashing Pumpkins, they also introduced me to the uniquely styled Jane's Addiction, thereby solving for me that mystery posed by the poster that had befuddled me during the haircut event described earlier.

I had yet to attend a live festival of this magnitude. People over twenty-five were rare at these events. I was well into my late forties and should have felt out of place. But I didn't. I was starting to take perverse delight in casually mentioning my interest—indeed, my commitment—to this kind of musical subculture to people my own age—friends, relatives, or professional contacts—and always drew amused bewilderment and feigned admiration from them. Attending Lollapalooza seemed to be absolutely mandatory as a step in completing my membership in this subculture. I wasn't pretending to be younger than my true age. I was just interested in being authentically confirmed, and this event would be my initiation. Naturally, I convinced Carmelo to go to Lollapalooza with me.

The event was held on a huge field in Stanhope, New Jersey. There would be alternative rock including grunge, eighties punk, electronic music, even hip-hop. This festival was conceived and run by Perry Farrell of Jane's Addiction. I was no longer a novice but rather, by then, a determined journeyman, with growing knowledge of the scene. We parked our car and made the short trek to the lawn, about the size of a football field.

Throngs of young people populated the field, some probably as young as my three teenage kids, some in their thirties, like Carmelo and his friends. I didn't see anyone in my age range, then forty-five. The field was surrounded by tent-covered stands and booths selling food, art, beverages, souvenirs, records, posters, and T-shirts from the ever-expanding universe of concert tees. There was an enthusiasm that I could not help from sharing with these young aficionados of music. The overall feeling at the time was that there was a new explosion of music that was exhilarating the younger generation. I was exhilarated myself even though I was two decades their senior.

Furthermore I had accrued considerable knowledge and enthusiasm for the so-called alternative music I was hoping to use as an antidote for dislocations that had occurred in my life during the years of my divorce. There would continue to be an enduring need for such from 1990 to 1995 and well beyond, for that's how long the legal process dragged on. Thus, it was always in the background of my experiences in those days. I was developing an almost obsessive interest in the music, which now came to be as personally important and fulfilling as my socializing at clubs and coffeehouses. I had been stunned, as well as intrigued, by the groundbreaking music video from Nine Inch Nails called "Head like a Hole." Therefore, I was looking forward to seeing them play live and in person.

I also wanted to see Siouxsie and the Banshees, because I was hearing so much of her band at the two clubs I attended. Furthermore, Siouxsie sported a look that was more glamorous and sexy than that of other punk rockers. She wore heavy mascara and blood-red lipstick. Her eye makeup had an Egyptian look like the Eye of Horus and appeared a bit sinister. I sensed that Souxsie's appearance was leaving the punk look behind and laying the groundwork for the style of Goth.

I wanted to see Jane's Addiction, the headlining band, which had a set of special connections for me since that first haircut in Paterson. But most of all, I wanted to experience these new-to-me bands.

As we set about placing a lawn blanket, we spotted a fellow Loop Lounge traveler named Laura. I had had the gumption to talk to her at the Loop despite the fact that she was taken by a tough-looking young man. Here, standing out on the grass under a bright sun, she looked the same as she did in the after-midnight world of the Loop. She was dressed in a black T-shirt, rendered sleeveless and faded, and skintight black jeans. Her pageboy hair was jet black, her eye makeup elaborate, her glittering armor of morbid-design medal-ware included mainly skulls on many rings and necklaces—the very image of Goth. Or was she, I wondered, from the punk scene? It gave me an insight into the genealogy of the music, and even the alternative music culture, which could be seen to trace its ancestry to punk of the 1970s and early '80s. She was here with the boyfriend that I had seen her with at the Loop.

Laura and her boyfriend greeted us with bracing sincerity. I felt confirmed in my growing theory that punk was the ever-evolving, overarching big-tent movement to which alternative and its various subcategories belong. The extent to which all the styles of alternative music draw from their punk ancestry varies greatly. Purists would reject this whole observation as undermining the separateness of each of these supposedly clearly identified categories.

As Laura and her friend went about their way, we settled into our lawn blanket. While doing so, one of Carmelo's friends from the Loop approached us. It was Artie, one of guys from the Iron-Bound and a particularly energetic, gregarious fellow who was about Carmelo's age. He had a photographic memory for concert events and the history of modern rock. He decided to settle with us, and we were happy to invite his company. He had much to say regarding the playbill and was familiar with all the performing bands at this Lollapalooza.

The day proceeded almost joyfully with this particular spectrum of music thundering out of colossal speakers. To my disappointment, Siouxsie and the Banshees had to cancel their performance for health reasons. I had understood them to be one of the early, foundational Goth bands. But I did get to see Living Colour, Butthole Surfers, and Nine Inch Nails, whose set that day provided me an education in the key elements of industrial music. I had been listening to their album *Pretty Hate Machine*, loaned to me by an acquaintance. One particular song from that album, "Down in It," contained an unsettling line that struck a chord with my situation. In it, Trent Reznor whines, "I was up above it… Now I'm down in it." Instead of taking this as sounding a cautionary note, I took it as a statement that I accepted and embraced my enrollment in this new subculture.

I was a little offended by Ice-T's vulgarity and hostility disguised as kind of aggressiveness that he shared with the audience. But I had understood from the beginning that in this scene—increasingly recognizable as survival of one of many elements of punk—there would be cutting-edge culture, elements of which might be less than pleasing. The tolerance intrinsic to the punk scene discourages negative value judgments, at least in theory. So I didn't let Ice-T's diatribe bother me or turn me off to the subculture in which he seemed to be an outlier.

More of that sought-after subculture was on display at merchandise stands where hot dogs and exotic foreign cuisine were served next door to the booth with challenging, harsh-themed artwork, another trait inherited from punk. In viewing the universe of concert tees, I realized that there was a hierarchy of prestige among the various bands, festivals, and concerts that the shirts commemorated, with older earlier acts like the Ramones rated highly. A glimpse at the names on records and CDs for sale was a review of the entire spectrum: the Cure, Psychedelic Furs, Depeche Mode, Alice in Chains, Henry Rollins, Living Color, and hundreds more. The more often I observed their name on a record package, the more success and prestige I imagined was attributed to them.

When the night drew toward the climax that would be provided by Jane's Addiction, everyone rose to their feet. We were situated well back in the field and had trouble seeing over the heads of the spectators that were beginning to form in the vicinity of the stage. Artie announced that it was time to move closer to the stage as Carmelo stayed behind to occupy the blanket.

I immediately noticed that the crowd was already dense, right where we stood, still many yards back from the stage. As I waded slowly into it, the density of the crowd in front of me grew with each step. Artie urged me on to move much faster so we could get as close as possible. It seemed to me, however, that we were already blocked from going deeper into the human mass. In front of us were people packed shoulder to shoulder. I was sure that there was no way to get closer. Artie was not in the least deterred. Pulling me along, he squeezed between spectators, again and again, layer by layer, penetrating the crowd in the direction of the stage. We moved between people so quickly, that we didn't even have enough time to voice polite apologies for forcing our way between them. Nor could we linger to address the gripes and threats from those whom we bumped and elbowed in the process.

Finally, we arrived at the chaotic front row, so we could see the whole show close up. While the stage was still waiting for Jane's Addiction to come on, a few of the spectators mounted their girlfriends on their shoulders. This, of course, obstructed some viewers; but surprisingly, few complaints were heard. More joined them.

It appeared to me that the human mass was beginning to act like a heated liquid. Squashed together mercilessly, some individual molecules of *Homo sapiens* squirted out above the tightly packed audience; and from there, they began crowd surfing, transported around by hands from below. At that point, Jane's Addiction burst thunderously on stage. Perry Farrell wore a flesh-colored woman's foundation garment, hugging him in elastic fabric from his ribs to a few inches below his hips where it ended with loose, flapping garter snaps dangling from the edge. The sight of him so attired added to the disoriented feeling that all viewers were experiencing.

When the song went into crescendo—electric guitar strings wailing and the frenetic chime-like strikes on a Caribbean steel drum—the crowd of spectators began to boil like the molten liquid that they constituted. More spectators were lofted up and out to form a kind of foam of crowd-surfers floating on top of the horde. Following the inexorable laws of fluid dynamics, just as liquid reaches the boiling point, a bubble formed in the crowd. Yes, despite the extreme density of the throng, somehow a circular gap about ten feet across burst into existence, with a few agitated young men, arms and legs flailing wildly, bounced off each other and off the circular wall formed by retreating humans, warding them off. They were engaged in the notorious slam-dance. Artie pulled me out to the perimeter of the bubble and, shouting to be heard over the din of music, warned me that I had just been pulled from the mosh pit.

Crowd surfers had splashed up onto the stage, whence they began diving back into the swarming mass of humanity, belly flopping onto the crowd, usually, but not always, without injury. This went on, repeated in waves and stages of boiling until the show ended. Jane's Addiction, the music, and the energy of the crowd—all these added up to an immersive, intoxicating experience that had exceeded my highest expectations.

When the performance was over, and the band bid us good night, the crowd began to disperse. We had gone deepest, right up to the stage itself, so we were the last to evacuate the area at the foot of the stage. The ground below us didn't bear any resemblance to a lawn. The sod had been pounded into slickness and was strewn with countless pieces of footwear. Slippers, sandals, and light sneakers were everywhere, stomped, of course, into distorted, flattened shapes like the ancient men retrieved from bogs and on display in a museum. Walking opposite direction to that of the exiting crowd, along came a young woman in dungaree shorts, staring downward as she walked toward us in front of the stage. She was scrutinizing the ground, trying to locate and salvage a missing shoe. On one foot she wore a completely unlaced Doc Marten type of ankle boot. The other foot was bare but for mud and soil that extended in streaks up her bare ankle to her shin.

My baptism into the scene was now complete. But I still hadn't sorted out the Goth vis-à-vis industrial elements. The lyrics of a Nine Inch Nails song "Down in It," which I had heard earlier, kept coming back to me, a jingle that kept repeating in my head: "I was up above it. Now I'm down in it."

A MOMENTOUS MEETING AT THE PIPELINE

During my solo visits to the Pipeline, I was deeply observant of the stark, highly cosmetic appearance and various styles of attire among the patrons. That was, after all, what had first caught my attention. My artistic efforts at painting in my home studio had not yet included denizens of this picturesque crowd, but I was looking for an opportunity to portray a stunning example in my art. So when I caught sight of a particularly attractive couple, I made it my business to introduce myself and become acquainted with them. I had recognized the man, who went by the name Myke Hideous and whose band had acquired certain notoriety under the name the Empire Hideous.

I had seen his band perform when I escorted my teenage son Johnny and his classmate to a show at the Bank, a nightclub where the Empire Hideous had been on the bill. Now, through sheer serendipity, I was face-to-face with the bandleader, Myke Hideous, and his wife. Myke wore a black wide-brimmed leather hat. The sides of his scalp were shaved clean, although a generous, relaxed ponytail trailed from atop his head and then down his back. His light-hazel eyes stood out from his swarthy, bony, and finely chiseled facial features. The all-black outfit was set off by dozens of little glittering pieces of chrome and silver jewelry: ear piercings, necklaces, and pendants that hung around his neck and attached to his garments in the form of spikes, buttons, zippers, and studs. I noticed he was wearing the same Army Navy store boots that I wore. I approached the glamorous couple and introduced myself as Doktor John and asked Myke to identify himself.

"Aren't you Myke Hideous? I saw your band perform a couple a months ago at a music hall called the Bank."

Myke seemed happy to have been recognized by an utter stranger, in this case, an older gentleman. I was impressed by the style of his elaborately groomed wife. She had costumed and made herself up to be the image of a seductive vampire, like one might view in a black-and-white B movie or as a character from a horror-comedy TV sitcom. Her appearance carried an element of parody, but it also bespoke true admiration for the prototype she was mirroring.

After I mentioned the show at the Bank, I asked about future performances of his band, the Empire Hideous. We talked about where we each had come from and what we had in common with the city of Paterson. As we chatted, I experienced the revival of an old ambition of mine: to create modern artworks that would be parodies of iconic paintings. My inspiration had been a series of museum-scale misrepresentations of famous paintings on display at a Greenwich Village theme bar called Night Gallery, one of the picturesque Eerie Pubs that were scattered around lower Manhattan during that era. As I gazed at the Hideous couple, I resolved to create work of art, a parody of Grant Wood's famous *American Gothic*. I would replace the farmer and his sister with the Hideous couple, and the farmer's held pitchfork with the head and neck of an electric guitar.

After some more conversation, I revealed myself as an amateur artist, and I proposed the artwork I had in mind. They accepted, and we set about exchanging phone numbers, addresses, and setting up dates for them to come to my pad to pose.

MYKE AND THE EMPIRE HIDEOUS

During the sessions spent photographing and painting the Hideous couple, we became increasingly acquainted, even friends. I gathered that growing up in Paterson, New Jersey, Myke had been influenced by a locally popular horror-punk band known as the Misfits. This group hailed from Lodi, New Jersey, and played a particularly harsh brand of three-chord punk rock. They had gained international notoriety for two specific reasons, in addition to their music. First, they were visually arresting with massive black pompadours that hung in a forward-falling tail, down the front of their faces. This coiffure was coined by the band and was termed a *devil lock.* They wore grisly *black* makeup, ringing their eyes, and costumed up in a retro mode that suggested a zombie version of Elvis Presley or doomed rockers performing in hell.

The second reason was that they were represented almost everywhere by a particular striking logo on T-shirts, posters, etc. It was the image of a face-on, macabre skull with little eerie eyes, incongruously placed within the eye sockets. The stark, lo-res white skull on a plain black background gave it a do-it-yourself punk flair. It turns out that this image was borrowed from the 1940s weekly cinema serial The Crimson Ghost. National and internationally famous heavy-metal bands like Metallica, et al. took to wearing T-shirts with this ghastly image when onstage, with the consequence of promoting interest and bestowing prestige on the Misfits.

Myke invited me to a special show at CBGBs, the new wave/punk club situated on the Bowery that had been instrumental in launching the careers of the Ramones, Patti Smith, Blondie, and the Talking Heads.

The event was one of an ongoing series dubbed *A Night of Misanthropy* and included performances by Loretta's Doll, Requiem in White, and The New Creatures. This series, *A Night of Misanthropy*, began in the very early nineties and took place at various downtown Manhattan venues including CBGBs.

Goth bands that rose to popularity in the New York greater metropolitan area during this era of the nineties, besides the Empire Hideous included Sunshine Blind, Rosetta Stone, and Sofia Run as well as out-of-towners the Wake. Under Myke's influence, I attended shows by all of them.

One of the most successful and enduring acts to emerge from this vibrant NYC underground, darkwave scene was Aurelio Voltaire, singer-songwriter, raconteur, stand-up comedian, and master of ceremonies. He served as emcee at many Goth events, warming the crowd with cynical humor, comical anecdotes; and with humorous songs, he wrote and sang, accompanying himself on guitar. In the era of the nineties, he went by the monomer Voltaire.

Before the Empire Hideous took the stage, they festooned the ceiling above the stage with hanging shrouds of gauzy linens, which, combined with dim lighting and machine-generated fog, created a creepy, otherworldly aura. He and his band wore tinted black lipstick, black eyeliner, and eye shadow. Myke wore his signature wide-brimmed black leather hat and took the stage by storm, roaring out a wall of darkly melodious, driving, rhythmic rock, which would have been mistaken by the unsophisticated ear as heavy metal. To me, the two styles now seemed worlds apart. The former was more creative, more musical, more original. The latter was a musical cliché.

When they topped the performance with the anthem "Power the Empire," I fully grasped the brilliance, creativity, and originality of the band and of the demonic genius behind it, Myke Hideous. The music of the Empire Hideous bore little or no resemblance to the simplified noise of the Misfits, but had fallen heir to their hell-bent, defiant attitude.

One might ask how and why I came to accept this dark, almost creepy aesthetic style. The most apparent underlying factor predisposing me to become comfortable with what is generally called the Goth scene was a lifelong affection for classic, early black-and-white horror cinema of the 1930s and '40s (i.e., the Universal Studios series including Frankenstein, Dracula, the Wolfman, etc.). I had grown up a fan of these films and everything that went with them since my earliest adolescence. I stayed up late nights with religious fervor, to watch these and other B movies on the family's twelve-inch fifties-era television set. The program host was a lovable, jocular character dressed and made up to resemble Lon Chaney's *Phantom of the Opera* from the silent era: hair parted in the middle with mascaraed eyes and sunken cheeks. He would have fit right into the scene in which I had chosen to become immersed. He was called Zacherley (1918–2016).

I knew I wanted to connect with this dynamic musical project and cooperate with it in any way that would further its success and deepen my involvement in the subculture. Chatting with Myke and with members of his female entourage, who resembled an updated version of Dracula's cinematic wives, I laid the groundwork for eventually becoming the band's manager and producing their next album. Myke emphasized the importance of a catchy nickname to be one's moniker within the scene. He dubbed me Doktor John.

After much in the way of rehearsals and studio time, our combined efforts turned out a compact disc called *Only Time Will Tell,* and I took credit as executive producer. Eventually, and many years and albums later, my finished portrait of Myke and his wife posed like the characters in Grant Wood's *American Gothic* came to serve as cover art for their final album *Remixes in Time.*

For several of the next few years, I made the Empire Hideous and my relationship with Myke an important facet of my new single life. This involved weekly or biweekly visits to their lair; attending rehearsals in order to familiarize myself with the band; developing relationships with its members; and picking Myke's brain for an overview of the local, regional, and worldwide Goth music scene. Myke became Vergil to my Dante as I embarked upon a trip to the underworld, the New Dark Age.

My Monthly Column, "New Dark Age"

Myke Hideous had written a regular column covering the NY/NJ dark music scene called Area 51 in the *Aquarian Weekly,* a rock music newsprint tabloid that had been around since the Age of Aquarius (i.e., Woodstock 1969). I had been contributing articles since 2001

under Myke's support and sponsorship, so it was natural that I should take over a similar role when he moved on. He landed me a position as a contributor under the auspices of the then editor, Chris Uhl. Chris was a prodigious authority on the current rock music scene and wrote brilliant articles that sparkled with insight and insider knowledge. Under his tutelage, I began issuing reports and record reviews that reflected Chris's guidance for concise, informative narrative, covering the myriad Gothic, punk, and industrial events (cultural as well as musical) that I would attend during the next two decades of my involvement. These came to include concerts, conventions, museum exhibitions, record reviews, newsworthy milestones, obituaries, and more. New Dark Age reports became the axis around which my life outside of medicine revolved. I signed each article as "Doktor John."

The first column I wrote was to cover the 2001 GothCon, a three-day convention of all things Goth, held in New Orleans. With this first entry into the world of journalism, my direction was set to delve mostly into the dark side, although that was by no means the only area I covered.

In the early days, I wrote about everything and anything that I attended and that might be of interest to the rock music community of New Jersey, the readership of the *Aquarian*. Since I had no interest in classic rock or heavy metal, my focus was on indie, antifolk, and alternative punk pop. As time went on, and my interest and commitment to the Goth-industrial scene deepened, my reviews took a decided turn in that direction.

Among the many interests I entertained, and about which I published reports in the *Aquarian*, were record releases by the uniquely creative metal band Tool and its spin-off project, A Perfect Circle. The themes and lyrics featured on their collective works bespoke the highly literate, if ferociously iconoclastic, mind of front man Maynard Keenan and resonated with my intellectual enchantment with the cultural anthropologic writings of Joseph Campbell and Camille Paglia. It was this kind of connection that I was to come across again and again as I roamed the "scene" in search of the next column I was to write. I came to realize that the dark music that drew my attention was to lead down numerous paths into literature, arts, and history.

Early in the 2000s, a venue that was a combination subterranean bar, the Lit Lounge, and art gallery, The Fuse Gallery, came into existence. The music offered up by the resident DJs was half hip as was the crowd that frequented the bar, but the gallery also featured some fresh and cutting-edge art by present-day artists. These included such notables as Winston Smith, whose sarcastic and surrealistic collages included illustrations for articles in *Playboy*, *National Lampoon*, and the *New Yorker* as well as cover art for the Dead Kennedy's album *In God We Trust*. A high point in The Fuse Gallery's brief glory was the exhibition of, and live appearance by, H. R. Giger, designer of the horror masterpiece *Alien* of cinema fame.

I made it my business, and with no tangible recompense, to attend every concert, music festival, and related museum exhibition to monitor every Goth/industrial record release, view every motion picture dealing with punk, and to read every review and write-up on the subject. This involved two or more times per week attending countless live band performances; reviewing new recording and rereleased collections; spending every New Year's Eve, Valentine, and Halloween at Goth bashes; attending weekly dance nights at various clubs, special-themed sailing cruises, live bands, and staged theatrical acts, film festivals, conventions ("cons") of all kinds, and several Miss Gothic NYC pageants. I was privileged to personally interview numerous celebrities from Mike Ness of Social Distortion to Peter Murphy of Bauhaus and myriad less-known artists.

As the new millennium unfolded, my mission began to declare itself: to chronicle the Goth-industrial culture and promote interest in it to the general rock music community. I called my monthly column "New Dark Age" in recognition of the resonance between this particular genre of music and the ongoing decline of Western civilization. The interconnectedness of underground music and decadence of society had been examined before, quite explicitly in motion-picture documentaries on punk (*The Decline and Fall of Western Civilization*) and metal (*The Decline and Fall of Western Civilization Part 2*). I felt I was witnessing part 3.

THE EMPIRE HIDEOUS

The Empire Hideous band formed in 1988 and was housed in a series of group homes, crash pads, and basement studios. A multi-talented artist, Myke Hideous was the central and indispensible core of the project as the lineup underwent constant turnover. He wrote the lyrics and music and staged the accompanying performance art, some of which was shocking and which I would have previously found objectionable. Like many teenage rock music fans in urban North Jersey, Myke was exposed to and interested in the horror punk genre as typified by fellow New Jerseyans, the Misfits. The Empire's style however came to more resemble the morose but melodious music of the Sisters of Mercy and Fields of the Nephilim rather than horror-punk.

In its heyday, EH produced numerous LPs, EPs, albums, two-band documentaries, and a multisong video album. Several magazines including *Propaganda*, *Ghastly*, and *Permission* interviewed Myke. The band's hit singles "Letters from Puppets," "Two Minutes to Midnight," and "Heaven's Raining Bullets" made the college radio charts. "Mr. Barnum," another single off the EP *This Evil on Earth*, was included in a significant compilation by the UK's Nightbreed Records. A serious following arose not only in the USA but the UK, Italy, France, Chile, Japan, Germany, Canada, and Poland. Several documentary films have covered the day-to-day activities as well as the professional careers of Myke and his band.

The Empire Hideous broke up and regrouped around Myke several times. In 1998 Myke was recruited as the lead singer for the by-now world-famous Misfits on an international tour. He returned somewhat disillusioned in his experience, but sprang back into musical side projects like SpySociety99 and the Bronx Casket Co. with longtime musician and production associates. In 2002, he revived the Empire Hideous, touring and staging performances. In 2004, Myke received an award as the "Best Goth Rock Front Man" (i.e., lead male vocalist) at a ceremony at CBGB's Gallery. In 2011, Empire Hideous released its last studio album of new material, *The Time Has Come*. In 2014, the album *Remixes through Time*, with reworked versions of older songs, was released with, at last, the image of my parody of Grant Wood's *American Gothic*, created twenty years earlier.

Despite numerous announced retirements of the Empire Hideous, the band never totally went out of existence. An abortive attempt to reinvent the project in the form of SpySociety99, a psychobilly, "death-lounge" band, didn't get far enough to eradicate Myke's lingering enthusiasm for the smoldering embers of his original band. Thus, Empire Hideous has undergone and continues to undergo repeated resurrections in the twenty-first century.

The band consisted of a collective of surprisingly gifted musicians who by and large lived communally in a series of temporary, usually basement, residential apartments. Tall, dark, and handsome, Jeff was a virtuoso guitarist with a charmingly ingenuous personality. He was to continue playing accompaniment to Myke through numerous reincarnations of Empire Hideous into the twenty-first century. The other guitarist—burly, outspoken, and an equally capable musician—went by the one-word name Mars. Periodically, Myke would ask me to "speak to" Mars about his punctuality and attendance at rehearsals. Left-handed bassist Eve LeStrange was quiet, good-natured, and seemed to have an alternate unspoken inner life. In years to come, and long after leaving the band, she was to become a prolific author of horror novels. Joey Quest played drums and sometimes violin, depending on the song's arrangement. He wore his long black Eurasian hair well down below the shoulders. He had a low-key, hesitant demeanor but was energetic in his instrumental delivery. Joey never seemed to mesh with Myke or the others and would eventually leave the band and be replaced by drummer Rafael Angel on drums.

The *first event* at which I served as manager was a performance at the famous Pyramid Club on Avenue A in the East Village. Myke and I met for a preliminary meeting there. It was my first time to this famous alternative nightspot. The Pyramid featured a bar that was attended by a whole variety of patrons, from Goths and punks to serious drinkers and regular "civilians." Myke introduced me to two women, the likes of whom I had never previously encountered. One was a slim, dark-haired beauty wearing a full-on black vinyl fetish outfit. The other was the formidable Miz Margo, who was to go on to become a bicoastal famous DJ and promoter. She wore tattered punkish attire, and her light-colored mohawk was coiffed into dreadlocks atop and behind her head. The sides of her head were shaved clean except for little curly sideburns that sprung out from her temples, just in front of her ears. She was the perfect virago. I offered to buy these two ladies a drink, but the vinyl-clad brunette declined.

"Don't worry. It's okay," Margo assured her companion. "He's not a weirdo."

I didn't grasp why the first woman harbored reluctance to accept a drink from me, but the other bolder Margo understood. I also thought it cute that these two really (from a conventional point of view) outlandishly outré women should worry about me—an average-appearing, middle-class, middle-aged day-crawler—might or might not be a weirdo. I had not been aware of the concern shared by many women in the bar scene, namely, that they might be slipped a date-rape drug. Margo could see through my motorcycle-jacketed façade to recognize a reserved and proper poseur who was neither a punk nor a threat of any sort. They both accepted the offered drinks.

Deep to the bar was a large dark dance floor crowded with day-crawlers dancing to seventies and eighties classics while they celebrated a bachelorette party. Down a steep flight of steps was the basement: dark, humid, and sparsely populated with Goths who danced earnestly to harsh industrial tracks, none of which I could identify.

A stage was available at the far rear of the upstairs dance floor where Myke's band was going to perform. Myke had negotiated the date with the Pyramid's promoter, DJ Jeff Ward who went by the title Father Jeff. The band was to perform the coming weekend.

When the night came for the performance, we gathered into a small backstage room in the basement where the band members tuned their instruments and applied makeup. Myke grew vehemently intense in his attitude, applying makeup that might have made Alice Cooper proud, shutting himself completely off from communication with the rest of us. Everyone knew not to disturb him in his efforts to focus with laser-like precision on the upcoming performance. At the appointed time, a trapdoor above us opened, and the instruments were handed up into the ground-floor stage as band members climbed up the ladder to set their positions on stage.

I enjoyed their great performance, as much, if not more than anyone in the audience, and swelled with pride to have served in a managerial role. In the long and checkered career of Empire Hideous, and through countless changes in lineup, they would perform at many festivals, balls, and shows. Myke, as a performer with the Misfits and as the lead singer in his several side projects, shared the stage with such notables of the genre as Black Sabbath, Sonic Youth, Marilyn Manson, Kraftwerk, and David J of Bauhaus.

Myke and I signed an agreement in which I was to manage the band. This involved securing opportunities to perform, talking to promoters, distributing show flyers, and making petty cash disbursals for ancillary equipment. I named my management company New Dark Age. Each time the band had to change living arrangements, we would pack, load, and transport the equipment, often with the help of fans who volunteered to do some of the heavy lifting. Then we would spend time stapling sound-proofing foam linings to the walls and ceilings of the rehearsal area in their new digs.

I eventually came to recruit a young friend, and world-wise councilor, Marty Coleman to serve as my assistant, actually, comanager. He had a deep knowledge of pop, rock, and alternative music; had a venturesome personality; and would later go on to become a minor celebrity, going by the moniker Mr. Haunt, self-identifying as a vulture of dark culture well into the twenty-first century. Together, Marty and I worked at managing and stage-managing the performances of Empire Hideous, assisting with the stage setup and controlling the stage props and lighting. The actual live shows were few and far in between in the nineties, but there always seemed some task or connection to be completed, some event to attend, some promoter with whom to connect.

The *craziest escapade* in which Marty and I participated on behalf of the Empire Hideous was one that combined our mutual interest in the band and horror movies. We caught word of a Fanex convention that was to take place in Towson, Maryland, over several days. Marty was never one to lack enthusiasm for a caper; so when the day came, I cleared my schedule, booked a hotel, completed application to set up a vendor's booth, and packed him and our Empire Hideous merchandise into my car. Along with CDs and VHS videotapes, I raided my office's orthopedic display models consisting of imitation bones and a long articulated spine dangling from a hook on a stand. An old TV monitor was placed on our table, running Empire Hideous music videos.

Although infrequent from my point of view, the Empire Hideous performances were always spectacles. On one occasion, Myke submitted to having hypodermic needles inserted into each of his eyebrows on stage to the horror and delight of the audience. For a Halloween performance at the Bank, he made an appearance dressed in a hospital jumpsuit, propelling himself in a wheelchair while acting feeble and demented.

Myke had a great deal of enthusiasm for one skit he performed in which he donned a cloth bag over his head like a person about to be executed by a firing squad and submitted to having a blank pistol fired at his head. It was always done with the utmost solemnity and suspense. Myke would prep me to stand by as a physician-in-attendance should this particular occurrence of the act result in an actual gunshot wound. This was more than a little disingenuous. My professional life as a surgeon dealt mainly with trauma involving broken bones and mangled limbs. I certainly would not have been in any position to treat a gunshot wound to the head.

One of my *favorite shows* Empire Hideous performed was at CBGBs and involved complicated and intentionally offensive stage props. An important characteristic of the Empire Hideous's style was to be transgressive, to delight in expressing Myke's signature style of artistic offensiveness. Besides being rhapsodic, sonorous, and musically grandiose, Empire Hideous also took on traits of a "shock rock," in the vein of Alice Cooper or Ozzy Osbourne.

For this effort, Myke had gone to a butcher and obtained two pig heads, which he mounted at the front of the stage on short poles à la *Lord of the Flies*. A couple of stylishly disheveled art-school punk girls had fabricated a television set having a chaotic eruption of electronic debris arching over its roof, as if the guts of the appliance had been vomited in a spray out its top. Myke placed a videotape showing disasters, tragedies, accidents, violence, and disturbing visual patterns on a continuous replay loop that ran during the musical performance.

On that occasion, I was assigned to man the table at the entrance of CBGBs and verify the proper tickets that Myke had printed up and the announcement flyers that served to grant entry. I was advised that there was a very important, supremely fashionable Goth couple who fully expected to be recognized on sight and let in for free and god forbid I should question or verify their identity, so universally famous as they were.

Indeed, just such a high-glamour couple did appear. The man was tall. His skin-tight tunic and pants showed him to be exquisitely thin. His shiny black hair was parted in the middle. His mouth, adorned with deep-purple lipstick, was drawn into a subtle, permanent, downward curve of scorn for anyone less beautiful or less haughty than he. He wore a light, slick black, ankle-length cloak.

His female escort was, if it can be imagined, even more stunning. She wore a black-on-black bodice with extra-long long sleeves over a floor-length, formfitting gown. There was crowded, intricate black lacing on all her garments. Her hat was a black fabric dome bedecked with an arrangement of identical silver beads in horizontal rows. Her fine facial features were spangled with numerous conspicuous, glittering nodes of metal piercings. A little chrome bead sat aside one nostril. Another sparkled from the shallow concavity in the front-middle of her upper lip. Two larger beads were partially sunk into dimples in her cheeks. Small hoops pierced her lower lip. Her eyebrows were adorned with rings that formed a neat little row below the brim of her hat. All this glitter seemed to flow in smooth continuity with that on her hat, like a chrome veil.

I wasn't supposed to stare, or they would know I was a day-crawler posing as a punk or Goth. Yet I couldn't stop trying to figure out where her face ended and her beaded hat began. I hesitated to let them pass. I asked who they were. This threw them both into a fit of indignation. Rather than answer, they demanded to know who I was to not recognize them and how could someone so out-of-the-know be placed in a position of screening people at CBGBs? I let them in. The band was already playing. No sooner had they entered than the beautiful/arrogant couple was bounding out, now with greater outrage almost to point of swooning or vertigo. Clearly, they were so choked with rage that they could not give voice to their fury.

It turns out that the beautiful/arrogant couple was hard-core, militant vegans, and animal rights activists that were brought to the absolute limits of what they could bear to witness when they beheld the severed pigs' heads. Was it the loathsome sight of meat to a pair of vegans that had caused for them the very zenith of offense? Or was it the presumption of animal cruelty to which these porcine fellow beings had been subjected? They flew past me without a word as they exited in a state of sputtering indignation.

For how famous they were supposed to have been, I never heard mention of the beautiful/arrogant couple ever again, and they remain unknown. Myke too remembers the incident, but their identities remain obscure to him as well.

THE CATHEDRAL

The first half-decade of the 1990s were a time of emotional and economic turmoil for me. It was during this five-year span that I found myself in the divorce process that was economically devastating and personally disorienting. I found myself consigned to a second-floor walkup above my medical office. The apartment consisted of four rooms, two of which were rented to a therapist, who used one as her waiting room and the other for treatment. I was confined to the two that remained. In the evenings after her office closed, I used her waiting room as my living room. This made for a cramped and constrained existence.

Since I was determined to make a much more active social life than my former situation allowed, I soon dislodged the therapist. At first, taking over all four rooms of the apartment allowed me to entertain a friend or two. But my involvement with the Empire Hideous and similar social contacts shortly resulted in the need for more space.

In 1995, I commissioned a large construction project on top of the existing apartment that resulted in two additional rooms. Besides an ample loft reachable by spiral staircase, there was added a mostly-glass great room measuring thirty-three feet by fifteen feet and an eighteen-foot peaked ceiling with skylights!

When the Empire Hideous performed live at the opening party for this new space, I began to realize its potential. Afterward, there would be a steady stream of garage-band performances on a mostly monthly basis. Every occasion for a party was exploited. My teenage son's punk band of high schoolers performed regularly, but the demographic was mainly young and middle-aged adults from the Loop and the Pipeline crowd. My comanager of the Empire Hideous, Marty, served as a kind of collaborator as event after event was scheduled. We called the great room The Cathedral, and I constructed a welcome sign that read "New Dark Age" under a stylized image of an eclipsed sun to serve as its logo.

Year-round Halloween became the theme of The Cathedral. Ghastly knickknacks, including a banjo-playing skeleton, a chrome skull-wearing wraparound sunglasses, and gargoyle statues served as the room's décor. A three-foot diameter wrought-iron globe hung high over the center of the room, and I installed two small flying gargoyles suspended from the ceiling on "invisible" wires.

Marty and I saw ourselves as trendsetters and entertainment hosts. Our Halloween parties were extravagant and enjoyed so intensely that I had to invent a theme for a follow-up celebration a month later. I called it Novemberfest. Restricting the consumption of alcohol and totally banning recreational drugs didn't put a damper on the attendance at live performances, concerts, and poetry readings.

Over time I became more involved in and familiar with the activities and interests of this expanding social circle. In turn, I tried to spread the word on cultural and aesthetic enthusiasms that linked with theirs. Weekly film viewings featuring classic black-and-white horror flicks and B movies took place each March, shown on a pull-down eight-foot screen. A typical double feature was the 1939 gem *Werewolf of London* with 1968 howler *Teen-Age Strangler*.

In an attempt at creative programming, one season (2007), the "film fest" brought together movies—good, bad, and indifferent—that featured dated cinematic gimmicks like goggle-facilitated, 3-D, and primitive color from the early days of cinema, before the advent of Technicolor. The thriller *House on Haunted Hill* required my rigging up my full-scale model skeleton to cross above the audience on a halting, squeaking clothesline to simulate the in-theater experience.

The most elaborate gimmick setup was called upon to turn *The Tingler* from 1959 into a powerful experience. When shown in theaters, there had been wiring of theater seats with vibrators that became activated during the climax when Vincent Price, onscreen, shouted to the audience that there had been an accidental release of the *Tingler* into the theater. For that, my engineer son, John, and I wired a row of metal folding-chair seats with door buzzers. We made sure that the most naïve and vulnerable viewers were seated there. Activating those buzzers at the climactic moment resulted in screams of fear and delight from the thrilled spectators.

The joyless and desolate prospect that my divorce had posed was spectacularly reversed. I embraced the new dark-tinged lifestyle with zest and enthusiasm. I was soon receiving mail from event attendees addressed to "Doktor John—The Cathedral."

The Countess

After several years, my involvement actually deepened, and I came to be recognized within the social circle of NYC Goths. I had begun dating a beautiful young doctor who I enjoyed bringing to scene events because she found them to be delightfully *outré*. She had acquired an interest in the mildly punk and postpunk music of the 1980s where she grew up in her native Poland. This served to soften the otherwise jarring experiences in which she would join me as we navigated this world of dark music. I came to call her the Countess.

The author as MC at Goth fashion show at the Limelight

She was a person with a definite affinity for novel experiences and quickly developed enthusiasm for the Goth scene. She was made to feel very much at home as my companion as a result to two chance experiences. Thus, when I was called upon to emcee and serve as the announcer of music events and fashion shows, the Countess came along with camera on hand and was treated to backstage sights and personalities that might have shocked a less open-minded observer. On one occasion, a pretty young man, while preparing to go onstage, to the Countess's astonishment, rested one foot on the arm of the sofa on which she was seated in order to facilitate donning his fishnet pantyhose. On another, she was invited to take photos of completely nude female members of the notorious punk band The Voluptuous Horror of Karen Black as they applied body makeup. The Countess treated these situations like she had been a dyed-in-the-wool denizen of the underground scene all her life.

Woodstock 1999

The Countess's involvement in the alternative music scene was deemed complete by our attendance, along with the circle of friends from the Loop Lounge, at the multiday outdoor music festival Woodstock '99. On the occasion of the thirtieth anniversary of the iconic and cultural pivot-point event, a 1960s-style massive gathering took place featuring many of the leading, popular alternative bands of the day.

The Countess and I and our friends packed into a capacious RV and made the trek to upstate Rome, New York, seeing the experience as perhaps the final hurrah of the musical scene of the 1990s. Names in the lineup that now have acquired the patina of "classic alternative" filled the playbill. Multiple stages, food courts, beer gardens, cyber cafes, medical stations, and, yes, a Tibetan monk chapel were distributed across dozens of acres of a former military base in Upstate New York. (Neither the original Woodstock, nor Woodstock '94, nor this Woodstock '99 actually took place in Woodstock, New York.)

Our group of friends split up, each tracking down their particular favorite performers, who ranged from the Offspring and Bush to Counting Crows, Metallica, and Willie Nelson. The Countess and I were ecstatic to see Dave Matthews Band, Sheryl Crow, Alanis Morrisette, and Jewel. At one point and in one location, the sound system failed, but generally, the presentations were technically excellent.

One of the bands we saw perform was Creed. We had been listening to their album on cassette for months before and enjoyed the in-your-face baritonal vocals that seemed to capture the grunge sound that epitomized late-nineties alternative music. Their appearance onstage came as a bit of a surprise in that the lead singer, Scott Stapp, didn't match the hard-core, pop-punk look we were expecting. I recall the Countess's expressed disappointment, noting that he wore a gold chain necklace and carefully groomed shoulder-length hair parted neatly in the middle, looking like a romantic lead in a TV soap opera. She had imagined, instead, a tough skinhead, such were her preferences and leanings in the new aesthetics we were both acquiring.

The most impressive artist, and most moving performance, was put on by Mike Ness, erstwhile lead of the punk band Social Distortion. Besides his powerful singing and the brilliant originality of his set (more traditional than Social D's oeuvre), his sincere and respectful relationship with the audience stood out amidst all the festivity and frolic of the massive multifaceted event. These qualities would be sampled many years and many performances later and were evident during a 2008 interview I was fortunate to conduct with him in my capacity as a reporter for the *Aquarian*.

Rather than going in the direction of punk, Woodstock '99 revived the hippie culture of the 1960s namesake event. Peter Max artwork decorated the main stage. Baked hemp cakes and cookies were on sale. In the July heat, many, if not most, girls went topless, some wearing body paint but most au naturel. Rain occurred sporadically during the three-day festival. Merry youths rolled in puddles, became coated with layers of mud, and then roamed in gangs to the amusement and shock of onlookers.

The grounds became increasingly strewn with litter. This litter consisted of light cardboard and paper food-carrying items that were discarded with abandonment after being used and wound up covering all the surfaces. This proved a serious issue when, during the closing hours of the festival, candles were distributed and lit to ward off the descending darkness at dusk. As the candles became unwieldy and undesirable to carry around, people began to set them on the ground where they eventually set fire to the scattered litter.

Our friends and the Countess and I made our way to the RV and packed to make an early exit. Other prudent participants also got into their vehicles and lined up for the procession out of the parking lot while the Red Hot Chili Peppers began their set. A rave, deejayed by Perry Farrell, was scheduled to follow and to run all Sunday night into Monday morning. As our RV made the slow, bumper-to-bumper crawl out, we looked back at the continuing festival and watched corners of it go up in flames.

RECURRING GOTH CLUB NIGHTS

As I moved from the mainstream pop music of young collegians and professionals, I reverted back to seeking the type of experience that I had discovered in my fan-relationship with the Empire Hideous. I had been primed long ago to appreciate the dark aesthetics from which the Empire Hideous had arisen. I was able to relate to a subculture where cemetery décor prevailed and women costumed themselves as vampires because of my affinity to old black-and-white horror movies. My memories of watching those classics from Universal and other studios from the early days of talkies were imbued with the delight that only a child or preadolescent experiences when delving into the ambiguity of semidarkness in the dead of night. Overcoming the—let's face it, negligible—fear associated with horror movies provides its own joy and the satisfaction of throwing off convention.

The naïve and unsophisticated audiences of the 1930s and '40s may have found these films frightening, even horrific. But in the jaded world of the 1950s and '60s, during which I devotedly watched them, I felt only fascination and affection. *Fond* is not nearly strong enough a word to describe my memories of staying up late, watching faux monsters and villains cavort on the tiny twelve-inch television set while the rest of the household was asleep. Many have said that what we learn with pleasure we never forget. Beneath my daylight persona as a dedicated physician and surgeon, a middle-aged bourgeois, I maintained a taste for the shadowy gloom of Gothic culture.

The most consistently accessible locations to immerse oneself in the Goth scene are the Gothic, punk, industrial dance clubs.

QXT's

Newark's famous venue, the Pipeline, the iconic and influential Gothic, punk, and industrial nightclub that helped slingshot me into the underground music scene, alas, closed in 1998. Meanwhile, that same year, a similar club a few blocks away was celebrating its seventh year of catering to much the same crowd. QXT's became heir to that subcultural thread, but proved to have much greater staying power. Although QXT's went dormant during the 2020 pandemic, that year it celebrated its thirtieth year of existence.

From the late nineties on, the Countess and I made frequent visits to QXT's adjacent to the Ironbound section of Newark. We made some friends among the regulars at QXT's and especially among the staff, including Damian, the entertainment manager and events promoter. We were also familiar with some attendees whom we knew from outside the club.

QXT's turned out to be the leading venue for Gothic, punk, and industrial music in the Greater New York metropolitan area. Founded in 1990, it was certainly the longest-running alternative-music venue until the pandemic lockdown hit in the early days of 2020. The club boasts three dance areas: a large laser-lit ground-level space where computer-generated mind-bending videos or classic eighties cinema are usually projected on screens overlooking the dance floor. This is where we did most of our dancing and socializing.

Often we would take the staircase down beyond a wrought-iron gate to one of the two subterranean bunkers. The first is Area 51, lit by sci-fi-style wall sconces and ceiling lasers. It is devoted to harsh electro-industrial music. We found that we could usually adapt to the ferocious sound level that fills this space pursuant to its mission of blasting out industrial-strength, hard-core techno. Strolling from Area 51 through a short corridor, we arrive at the Crypt, a dimly lit and atmospheric space where dark postpunk is usually heard. All three areas have adequate bar facilities and feature expert music staff alternating with celebrity guest DJs.

QXT's owes much of its uniqueness to entertainment manager and events promoter Damian Hrunka, whose moniker is Damian Plague. Affiliated with the club since the 1990s, Damian has lived far and wide, picking up knowledge and interests in the Netherlands; Belgium; and the German city of Bayreuth, famous as the epicenter of Wagnererian Opera, even to this day. During his European adventures, he signed on as keyboardist for the ultradark, death-art band Das Ich with which he frequently goes on tour. We always knew that when Damian was away, that's what he was doing.

Damian also forms a link to the defunct, but once highly influential, Montclair, New Jersey, record store Café Soundz (run by Bobby Lisi, the DJ from the Pipeline), where he met and formed relationships with DJs and promoters from all around the metro area and the world. Thus, Damian remains QXT's top-level contact for bringing in such internationally famous performers as Covenant, Assemblage 23, Hocico, and Suicide Commando.

In addition to the massive role Q's played in the dance and live music scene, it has been the venue for many organizations and their special events like burlesque shows, Iron Garden, art exhibitions, meetings of *NJ Pagans* and *Sanctuary* magazine celebrations among others. We generally went to these special events, including live shows by all of the above-mentioned internationally known bands

Q's also hosts multiday festivals, promoting awareness of styles and movements within the alternative music scene, like the Synthwave Festival, at which we got to hear and familiarize ourselves with rising stars of this sub-subgenre. Synthwave is, of course, the wing of electronica that creates and composes music which echoes the soundtracks of eighties-era action and sci-fi/horror flicks. Who'd have known? Well, after attending and really *digging* (to use a sixties term) the Synthwave stars, we were now in the know.

Q's (as those familiar refer to it) also hosts art exhibitions, meeting spaces for off-beat organizations like Iron Garden ("A safe haven for New Jersey's Nightkind Community") and merchandise stands for artisans hawking dark crafts and *objets d'art.*

Learning about expressions of the avant-garde was a lifelong pursuit for the Countess and me; and it took us to many venues, not just museums and libraries, but to real-life, flesh-and-blood encounters with creators in the chaotic world of underground arts. The main benefit seems to be that, in doing so, one gets to learn to like a lot of diverse things, not just the laundry list of conventional likes that average people tend to have.

QXT's Special Event

We were always on the lookout for special, quirky happenings. One such event was the *Sanctuary* magazine's fifth year anniversary party at QXT's. *Sanctuary* magazine is mainly a photography journal featuring glamorous Gothic and fetish models. It contains interviews, profiles of artists and models, announcements and articles relating to underground lifestyle and events. The anniversary party was filled with mysterious, intriguing, and seductive creatures.

It shouldn't surprise the reader that entertainment included a shibari artist and the really raunchy performance by agro-industrial duo Hot Pink Satan, during which gorgeous and wanton vocalist Clea Cutthroat got down to very little clothing and even lost her platinum blond wig. A procession of candle-bearing models was followed, first, by a reading given by the grand dame Madame X and then a pagan ritual provided by Madame's organization, Iron Garden.

Just as regularly as we would attend QXT's, we also sought out nightclub-based events in NYC. Regular club nights like Necropolis at Windfall and The Red Party at Mercury Lounge became two of the most prominent dance parties to attend. There were certainly others, some iconic, like Defcon and the No Return Post Punk Society at the Pyramid. The Pyramid eventually failed due to Covid restrictions. What is known at this time is that the No Return Post Punk Society has moved to Brooklyn.

Necropolis and Father Jeff

Towering figure of the NYC Goth scene, Father Jeff Ward has achieved his stature by organizing, hosting, and deejaying some of the best attended and longest-lasting club nights. Prior to the 2020 lockdown, his flagship monthly event Necropolis was a must-attend event for the glitterati of the Manhattan demimonde. Father Jeff began deejaying at The Bank, which was then newly opening. In the years that followed, he has been a fixture at most, if not all, Goth dance clubs in the Greater NYC area and beyond. Hosting Necropolis, Father Jeff always curated the opening soundscape, knowing just when to play a classic track, like one by Sisters of Mercy, and when to insert tracks by recent artists or those who had little exposure, keeping us up-to-date on alternative music.

In addition to Necropolis, Father Jeff also produced the time-honored and recurring event, Ward 6, a dance night that shared its name with a short story set in a mental asylum by Anton Chekhov. All of his events were known and revered for the diverse and comprehensive musical set lists, which each DJ brought to the turntables, consistently mixing beloved eighties Gothic and industrial classics along with the latest EBM imports and B-side rarities. Every track seemed selected for compelling danceable rhythm.

Necropolis took place on the first Saturday of every month. It was held at Windfall, a restaurant by day that transformed into a dance hall by night and once served as an elegant meeting hall for the local Architect Guild. The setting was elegantly capacious, with a quiet corner and a familiarly friendly gatekeeper just inside the entrance. The bar was long enough to accommodate imbibers to gather socially without crowding. The end of the room nearest the entrance provided a quiet niche where low and intimate conversations could be held. Windfall host Chris Savo oversaw the festivities at each event with dutiful attention to the comfort and safety of his guests.

Necropolis represented a revival of the antecedent Jeff Ward event Necromantik that had been housed in the downtown Knitting Factory until that venue relocated to Brooklyn. Its first relocation of Necromantik had been to Element, formerly The Bank, but that too had closed, paving the way for Father Jeff to resettle Necromantik—under the name change, Necropolis—to Windfall for a nine-year residency ending with the pandemic of 2020.

Just about every active participant and creator in the NYC Goth scene attended Necropolis, some often, others occasionally. Horror/sci-fi publisher Derrick Hussey was always interesting to engage in conversation alongside the bar at Necropolis. He also made us aware of the Necromicon Festival of Weird Fiction. He made it sound intriguing, but neither the Countess nor I are big fans of fiction, and being skeptics, we have a lot of trouble suspending disbelief for stories with spiritual events that are outside the realm of the scientifically plausible. On the other hand, we really love both good and not-so-good cinema based on sci-fi and horror and find it easy to suspend disbelief if the motion picture is top quality as far as acting, sets, scenery, and cinematography.

No report on Necropolis—or for that matter, The Red Party—is complete without mention of the omnipresent, taciturn, pencil artist Bill. Dressed in a beret and sporting a long gray ponytail, Bill is a steady fixture at all such events, sketching away to the dim light of a flashlight, peeking outward occasionally to capture a glimpse of his models: the dancers and barflies that populate whatever venue he has chosen to inhabit for the evening. Bill seems to follow a strict set of rules. When being spied upon by those curious about his artwork, Bill shuts down his flashlight to prevent observation of his handiwork. Bill also strictly avoids all conversation unless engaged by members of the fair sex.

Necropolis boasted a lineup that included three famous DJs: Erik Aengel; Sean Templar; and Patrick Cusack, one of NYC's most respected DJs owing to his knowledge of musicology and his personal style.

DJ Patrick holds a special place in the NYC Goth scene. Patrick is identifiable for his signature style: black suit jacket over a black shirt and tie, topped by his shaggy mop and tinted spectacles as he circulates among patrons and fellow DJs between sets. His meticulously Goth apartment décor reveals the same attention to style so that his room resembles nothing so much as a miniature museum or tiny cabinet of curiosities featuring a bearskin rug, antique books, a fierce leopard skin, a sculptural tombstone, etc.

He began deejaying back in third wave of postpunk, or what he called the big Goth revival in the early nineties. Patrick's ideal has been, from the beginning, to introduce the newest bands and songs alongside the eighties standards. He stuck with that paradigm since his first gigs as a DJ during the big Goth revival of the 1990s, nurturing it throughout his long and varied career, upholding this model in helping shape the NYC underground dance music scene.

"I have no interest in spinning 'Temple of Love' for the millionth time," says Patrick. Going on, he adds, "Those who do should just work weddings."

Patrick was about to celebrate twenty-eight years as a DJ when the Covid lockdown came. He has deejayed twice at the Wave Gotik Treffen in Leipzig, Germany, and annually at the Murder of Crows Festival in New York. He has spun at shows featuring Clan of Xymox, London after Midnight, Lycia and the Wake. Spinning for Rosetta Stone resulted in his selection to serve as USA manager, establishing a close connection with Cleopatra Records, such that he was instrumental in getting the Wake and Children on Stun signed to that famous record label.

How did this all come about? Growing up in Paterson, New Jersey, Patrick was a fan of the new wave, naming Devo, Missing Persons, and the B-52s as typical of the kind of bands in which he was interested. The Cure and Siouxsie and the Banshees were new wavers that transitioned him into a darker version of the wave. Seminal albums released in 1985, *The Head on the Door* by the Cure, *First Last and Always* by the Sisters of Mercy, and *Love* by the Cult pulled Patrick deeper into the darker depths of new wave. He began dressing all in black but didn't recognize a name for the style. He doesn't recall widespread use of the term *postpunk* in those early days. One day, while reading an interview of Siouxsie, he had an epiphany. He was introduced to the term *Goth*, and it clicked.

What prepared Patrick for a plunge into the dark side of popular music? More than most of his peers, in growing up, he had enjoyed the wry humor of the *Addams Family* and *The Munsters*, both of which delivered tongue-in-cheek favorability of what had previously been thought of as detestable monsters of cinema and literature. He also liked straightforward horror motion pictures. He discerned that his newfound taste in Goth rock fit well with his peculiar appreciation of the aesthetics of cemetery landscapes.

As his interest in personal interior home décor grew, Patrick found ample inspiration from his growing taste in music and entertainment in general. Increasingly, he found himself more and more at home within his own home, which he outfitted with furnishings and ornaments having a Gothic flare.

After developing and then losing interest in such bands as the Cult and Fields of the Nephilim, Patrick came to favor newer bands like London after Midnight, The Wake, and Rosetta Stone. He regularly attended a night called Troublemaker at Mother in the Meatpacking District and began bringing his own records for DJ Reese to spin. One of the promoters, DJ Craig, asked Patrick to deejay at his new party night he was establishing at the Pyramid club.

In regard to the dreadful year 2020, Patrick states, "Covid has obviously put a damper on all club related things. The night I deejayed at Necropolis the first week of March before everything shut down was my twenty-eighth anniversary as a DJ in Manhattan. Windfall, where Necropolis took place, has now closed for good. So I have no idea what will happen next. I'm grateful that I had a great run if it ends up being over."

Patrick's all-time favorite bands include Devo, Christian Death, Sisters of Mercy, the Cure, and American pop-rock duo Sparks.

Necropolis Attendees

Diana and Jill

Other luminaries that we encountered at Necropolis included DJs Arsenal and V-Christ. Impresario Sir William Welles was approachable and an interesting conversationalist, usually at the far end of the bar. I'd never fail to mention how valuable a service was his regularly updated New Goth City website that served as a directory of Goth events, sights, sounds, and points of interest. Goth vamps and Goth punks made up the basic population of Necropolis.

Diana and *Jill* were always to be found at Necropolis, dancing in a dark corner just off the DJ's booth. Diana is such an exemplary inhabitant of the Goth scene that she can serve as a template for countless other similarly inclined New Yorkers. She entered at age twenty-five in the early eighties when punk was transitioning into new wave. The dark aesthetics of Goth appealed to her individualistic, introverted personality and her taste in art, architecture, music, literature, theater, and fashion. Because of her fondness for the night, the moon, graveyards, churches, Halloween, and supernatural creatures like witches and vampires, she began dressing in Victorian funeral attire and wearing dark theatrical makeup. She loved viewing similar-looking guests from the shadowy corners of bars and nightclubs where she took up residence on a weekly basis.

Diana found contentment in the ethereal, gloomy, yet exhilarating dance music she heard at nightspots and concert halls in and around NYC and was spiritually lifted up by dancing along with kindred spirits of the scene. Eventually, she was spending much of her free time at dance clubs and small performance spaces on her native Long Island and the iconic venues of NYC like the Limelight, The Ritz, Webster Hall, Roseland, Hammerstein, Irving Plaza, and Williamsburg Music Hall. Diana's recollections comprise a compendium of places and events that cover virtually every and all activities in the NYC Goth scene for the past thirty years.

She danced at the Bank, the Batcave, Green Door, Coney Island High, Pyramid Club, and even QXT's in NJ. Diana's recent favorite hangouts included Necropolis at Windfall, the R Bar, Talon Bar, the Red Party at Mercury Lounge, Bowery Electric and Otto's Shrunken Head. For live performance concerts, she attended Jones Beach Theater, the Highline, the Beacon, Gramercy, Knitting Factory, Bowery Ballroom, St. Vitus, and Le Poisson Rouge.

Diana cherishes the memories of having attended Endless Night Vampire Balls in NYC, New Orleans, and Tampa; Dark Side of the Con; Redrum Balls; and Dead of Winter Festivals at Revolution Bar on Long Island.

In addition, Diana frequented such death/dark-themed places like the Beetle House, the Bodies Exhibit, Obscura Antiques and Oddities, the Dungeon, and the Museum of Death in New Orleans. She holds in high esteem the many talented DJs of the NYC area for playing the music of her favorite bands like Clan of Xymox, Seabound, Fields of Nephilim, The Mission, London After Midnight, Joy Division, Bauhaus, the Cure, Diary of Dreams, and Bella Morte. Diana also expresses her love for the works (in no particular order) of Edgar Allen Poe and Charles Addams (the Addams Family) as well as the cinematic efforts of Tim Burton, Bela Lugosi, Alfred Hitchcock, and Christopher Lee.

Diana was extremely saddened by the closures put into effect to control the pandemic of 2020 and wondered if it portended the end of the subculture in which she had been immersed. She expressed determination to go on experiencing Goth subculture in whatever ways it may survive. Diana continued to listen to the musical genre to which she had long ago become committed. She set about hosting small-scale dance nights on her patio adorned with candles, dim lights, and cardboard stand-ins for dance partners. On such occasions, she dressed in Goth attire with one or two friends and danced to darkwave music on YouTube or livestreamed by their favorite DJs on Twitch. She even attended the live stream of Endless Night Halloween Ball from New Orleans. Her commitment seems extreme, but it is only one of many examples of similarly motivated denizens of the NYC underground music scene.

The Red Party

DJ Sean Templar

The famous recurring monthly Red Party, hosted by master impresario DJ Sean Templar with hospitality hostess, photo-archivist, and Red Queen M Banshie is an event that was about to celebrate its twelfth year before the pandemic-related shutdown. In addition to local and regional acclaim, Templar enjoyed international renown as a DJ at the annual Wave Gotik Treffen, hosting his own signature style dance night called When We Were Young.

The Red Party was ever a good place to meet up with friends sharing our musical tastes, and to hear excellent dance tracks and do a little surveillance of the Lower East Side / Soho street scene. Late night snacking at Katz's historical deli often topped off the evening before we would head home or to our hotel.

The Red Party has been knocking around NYC since 2007. While it originated at a dedicated Goth club at 200 Orchard Street, and some occurrences took place at le Poisson Rouge, the final residence became the Mercury Lounge on East Houston, adjacent to the defunct Bank/Element Club.

Sean Templar heads the list of DJs with Jarek Zelazny, who usually took over later into the night. There are, of course, guest DJs like Matt V Christ, Ana Vice, and Valefar Malefic. The music served up by this panel tends toward deathrock and all the varieties of post-punk, darkwave, and Goth.

As soon as we would walk in, especially when we were early, Sean and the Mrs. would greet us, but right away he would head to the DJ spot on the stage. Sean is a strikingly handsome guy. Well, in that regard, one morning his Mrs. posted a profile photo of Sean on Facebook. I was so impressed not just by how beautiful his facial features were but by how profoundly iconic was his image, coiffed as he was in a semi mohawk. I was so inspired that I undertook to create a portrait of Sean in oil on canvas. When it was completed, the portrait painting was ceremoniously placed on display at the next Necropolis event where Sean was spinning; and his spouse, M Banshie, was gatekeeper.

Most Red Parties include live acts from the greater NYC area, the rest of the country, the UK, and around the world. There are several special editions of the Red Party that occur during the year. The Red Party that occurs in the Valentine's season is called The Love Will Tear Us Apart Ball, expressing ambivalence toward love as coined by Joy Division in their most popular song. Once or more times per year, the night is titled Welcome to the Reptile House, and is heavy with the music of The Sisters of Mercy. There are also New Year's Eve parties termed Forever Young, which usually start after midnight, making them actually New Year's Day parties. The recurring night dedicated to the repertoire of Joy Division is termed The Atrocity Exhibition.

We attended the Red Party almost monthly for several years, privileged to see and hear live performances by great local and international talent. A sampling included Goth metal giants the Empire Hideous; the Long Losts, a husband-and-wife duo performing over-the-top salute to horror television and cinema; Tiers, a Brooklyn trio playing morose melodies on boards, electric drums and guitar; and countless more, many equally memorable bands.

When we would enter the Mercury Lounge, we would always stop by the bar at its nearest point to the entrance door. There we would hope to find George Grant, revered music professional of the scene, wearing his derby hat and accompanied by his industrial-music-fan wife, Toni.

Red Party Attendees

George Grant grew up in Pittsburgh where he worked in a record store that expanded his horizons into the realm of alternative music.

Like many who later turned Goth, he began with a fascination for the glam rock band KISS and its bass-playing front man Gene Simmons. Drawn to the bass guitar for practical reasons, George found inspiration in other bassists besides Simmons, namely, Geddy Lee (Rush), Chris Squire (Yes), Geezer Butler (Black Sabbath), and Steve Harris (Iron Maiden) and soon was playing with many bands. After moving to NYC, he began frequenting clubs like the Limelight, the Bank, Long Black Veil, and the Batcave; and he came to admire the curating skills of such DJs as Jason from Alchemy/Absolution and Sean Templar.

George also started fidgeting with sound recording, employing the primitive technology of the time, namely, two audio cassette recorders, which he used to overdub himself and bandmates. Eventually, he moved his sound recording efforts into recording studios but found that to be too expensive, so he set about to eliminate the middleman, obtaining the needed equipment and setting up his own studio. Soon he was recruited to coproduce numerous albums with various artists, employing his signature style of "sonic collage."

He entered the Goth scene in earnest when he was tapped to play bass and coproduce an album with Aurelio Voltaire. George went on to serve in the same dual capacity for five more Voltaire albums and numerous live shows. In addition, George has a foot in the horror-punk genre with his band the Serpenteens, which produced three albums in the 2010s, currently in hiatus. He also plays, writes, and performs as vocalist as well as bass guitarist in various other styles of rock including metal, power pop, soul, and electronic. His one dislike? Jazz.

George rounds out his Goth experience and identity by attending major events and festivals like Dragon Con, Endless Night in New Orleans, Murder of Crows in Brooklyn, and of course, Wave Gotik Treffen in Germany to which he paid a much overdue visit in 2019.

As a respected producer and performer, George's taste in music says a lot. His favorite Goth bands include Bauhaus, Fields of the Nephilim, the Cult, Sisters of Mercy, and the Mission. He makes the distinction of separating these from his postpunk faves New Order, the Wire, and newer up-and-comers Hapax, Delfine Coma, Bootblacks, and Actors. At the time when we last checked up on George, he was experiencing overwhelming praise and success with his latest creative project, *Black Rose Burning*, impossible to classify but with elements of Goth, synthwave, rock and more.

After catching up with George and inquiring about his latest efforts, we generally moved through the bar area, through the double doors, to the dance floor in back. There, Sean was seen up on the stage, manning the computerized turntables and theatrically conducting whatever song he was playing with outstretched arms while lip-syncing at the top of his lips. Scanning the crowd of glamorous Goths, we sought out the friendly companionship and conversation one of our favorites and a regular at most Red Parties, Jen.

Like us, *Jen* is a regular at clubs and Goth cultural activities. An attractive and stylish lady in her fifties, who appears ten years younger than her stated age, Jen grew up around Chicago and conveys a distinctively Midwestern aura that distinguishes her in the NYC scene.

In her teen years, she took up playing the keyboard and was simultaneously drawn to the then-prevalent punk style, musical and otherwise. Around then, punk rock was losing its novelty and being replaced by so-called postpunk style. Appreciation of bands like the Cure and Depeche Mode led the way for her and her high school friends to transition while holding on to the counter cultural, "alternative" aesthetic that set them apart from their more conventional peers. Her friends labeled her "deathrocker," a nickname that still bemuses her. In college, Jen associated with the artsy, bohemian crowd and eventually moved to an edgy, chic neighborhood. There she absorbed some of the lingering new-age hippie culture with its interests in Eastern mysticism, psychedelics, and liberal politics. She began attending shows. In 1990, she attended a performance of Nine Inch Nails at Cabaret Metro, injecting the subgenre "industrial" into her developing musical taste and personal interests.

During a trip to London in the early nineties, Jen became aware of a distinct Goth scene and identity. When she moved to NYC in

1993, for what was supposed to be a six-month graduate program, she immediately sought the Goth scene out and soon developed friends at clubs like the Bank, the Batcave, and the Limelight. She decided not to return to Chicago and has been deeply embedded within the NYC postpunk culture since then and has dated several prominent figures who, like Jen, were regulars of the scene. She has applied her musical talents to serve as keyboardist on several bands, deepening her involvement and identity with the NYC circle, which is, after all, based on alternative music.

Like many in this subculture, Jen has stepped back from the Goth social scene on a few occasions. Pursuit of spirituality, leading her to Tibetan Buddhism was one such basis for taking a sabbatical from the scene. Bearing children was another. But like so many others, Jen returned with renewed commitment each time. Perhaps her several pilgrimages to the annual Wave Gotik Treffen have grafted an irreversible Goth identity on to her psyche.

As soon as COVID restrictions were eased, The Red Party came roaring back in July of 2021, starting anew with a new-wave/eighties themed event at its home, the Mercury Lounge.

No Return Post Punk Society and Roe Poalino

The Pyramid Club was the starting point for my involvement with Myke and the Empire Hideous. The downstairs space usually hosted various dark dance music including Defcon and the No Return Post Punk Society. The latter has maintained a reputation as a friendly, all-welcoming Goth party with no dress code and a campy, fun feeling. It first debuted in 2014, with first-time DJs Ryan Walker and Nancy Wolfe. "No" stood for Nancy and "Return" for Ryan. They ran it as one-off gigs here and there around town for a few years, intended as a Sunday happy hour for college friends. They were joined by Janssen Huayamave as a partner and, eventually, DJ. A cult following developed, and Ryan landed a regular night at the Pyramid club. Emily Smykal took on the dual role of hostess and DJ. She recruited in Alex von Nihil, who brought a quirky sense of humor as the third and final resident of the NRPPS. Alex von Nihil, outwardly happy and renowned for hospitality, took his own life in 2018. The NRPPS held multiple parties in his honor and memory with proceeds going to the American Foundation for Suicide Prevention. Thereafter, Janssen and Ryan continued as "dueling DJs" at the Pyramid before the pandemic lockdowns, and then persevered, first on twitch.tv and, as of this writing, have relocated to Eris Evolution in Brooklyn.

Roe Poalino came on to serve as hostess and photographer. Her personal story is an epic journey through the entire Gothic, punk, and industrial landscape, an odyssey that begins with new-wave music and dark-cult interests and takes her from Philadelphia Punk to the NYC Goth club scene.

Roe Poalino grew up in Philadelphia and her adolescent interests were music and photography. Another early enthusiasm was for the cult soap opera *Dark Shadows*, which she watched faithfully daily after school, a stark contrast with the virtuous values and righteousness to which she was exposed in Catholic elementary and high school.

Roe was not interested in disco or the then-prevalent rock music on the radio, preferring the throwback sound of The Rolling Stones to which her older sister had introduced her, as early as age eight, and played for her on vinyl 45s and 33rpm albums. She especially appreciated the more rebellious songs like "Sympathy for the Devil" and "Satisfaction." Her taste in music came to include Elton John, the up-and-coming new wave, Bowie, and Roxy Music.

Roe made a regular hobby of filling a scrapbook with photos of her idols, the Rolling Stones, clipped from rock music periodicals. These magazines sometimes featured punk rockers from New York and London. Their music was not being played on commercial radio, and Roe was too young to attend live performances. As a result, she developed a fascination for what was then out of her reach and began to fantasize about the bizarre hairstyles, the tattered clothes, and motorcycle attire—the energy and rage it seemed to embody.

A month shy of her twenty-first birthday, Roe was invited to accompany a music-enthusiast friend to the Hot Club, a former jazz joint on South Street in Philly, to see the Dead Boys. In between acts, the DJ played punk rock like Sex Pistols and 999 on a 45-rpm turntable. The novelty had her returning every Monday and Tuesday, the nights given over to the new music she found so exhilarating.

Eventually, she would see performances by Richard Hell and the Voivoids, Elvis Costello, Talking Heads, Devo, the Cramps, and more at the Hot Club. In 1978, she stood disappointed on line waiting for a performance that never took place because Sid Vicious was arrested that day for the murder of Nancy Spungen. In 1980, she and her friends took a ride to New York and saw New Order, recently reorganized after the death of Ian Curtis earlier that year. She never went anywhere without her camera, capturing the bands, the patrons, her friends, and the good times. She filed a collection of ticket stubs with her photos and began to amass a large collection of vinyl records.

She lost touch with her Philadelphia club-scene friends when she moved to NYC and soon took a government job, residing in Greenwich Village. For the interview, she had worn a Princess Diana wig to disguise her spiked platinum blond hair. Lonely and bored, and unfamiliar with the NYC club scene, she didn't return to her passion for music listening and live shows until two years later. But eventually, she began attending concerts at venues like the Palladium, The Ritz, Roseland, the Limelight, and the Fillmore for performances of the Creatures, Ian McCullouch, PiL, Peter Murphy, Ministry, KMFDM, Sisters of Mercy, and the Cure.

All this while Roe still had scant notion that a NYC Goth subculture survived. For her, punk rock and new wave, postpunk, and Goth seemed a casual transition from her earlier years as a fan of The Rolling Stones and glam rock. She began to notice that at Goth performances, people dressed the part.

In 2010, an old acquaintance she remembered from Philadelphia, Tim Mullen, noted electrical engineer/collector, invited Roe to "something going on in the Goth scene." She had assumed that "the Goth scene" had faded away many years earlier. Together they visited Don Hill's on the far west side of Soho. Roe was enthralled by the dim, blue lighting, and the black-clad crowd dancing a distinctive shuffle. She felt a much-needed reconnection with her former identity. The experience brought Roe deep into the postpunk scene. She felt like she was living within the movie *Dusk Till Dawn* as she danced to The Sisters of Mercy, the Cure, Joy Division, the Smiths, and The Cult.

Together, she and Tim attended Underworld, a dance night at Sullivan Hall, Dark Water at Otto's Shrunken Head, and Contempt at the Delancey where there were three floors of Goths!

In 2011, she met an influential friend at Carnival of Souls, Michael Kennedy, who knew all the events to attend and who turned Roe on to bands like VNV Nation and Wolfsheim. She broadened her attendance at clubs to include QXT's in Newark; Arkham in Brooklyn; City of Dark Angels; Ward 6 at the Bank (later Club Element) in downtown Manhattan; Necropolis at Windfall in midtown; Cybertron and Stimulate at Drom on Ave A; Defcon at the Pyramid, Procession at Home Sweet Home; Redrum Ball at the R Bar; and at various events at the Bowery Electric, Santo's Party House, and the Gramercy.

Along the way, she landed a role in photographing and hosting the No Return Post Punk Society at the Pyramid on Avenue A.

In the heyday of the NYC Goth scene, Roe could be found taking in the performances and taking pictures at any of the following venues, besides all those mentioned above, plus the Mercury Lounge;

St. Vitus; Brooklyn Bazaar; Warsaw; Elsewhere; Brooklyn Steel; and her home away from home, the No Return Post Punk night at the Pyramid. Why? She found that the depth and darkness of the music comforted her, sustained her, and acted as a painkiller.

When the Covid-19 pandemic passed, Roe looked forward to recurrences of Jet VF's Darkside of the Con, Sean and M Banshie Templar's A Murder of Crows, and meetings at Madame X's Iron Garden.

Roe's taste in music and affection for various bands has grown to vast proportions and includes all the classic postpunk Goth bands like the Cure, Siouxsie and the Banshees, Simple Minds, Sisters of Mercy, and Joy Division. Her all-time industrial favorites include Covenant, Icon of Coil, Killing Joke, Nine Inch Nails, and VNV Nation. Roe also continues to follow side-project soloists from the classic era like Peter Murphy; Peter Hook; and Gary Numan; as well as postmillennial, less-easily classified groups such as She Wants Revenge, The Exploding Boy, The Actors, The Rope, Cruxshadows, The Editors, and Interpol.

City of Dark Angels

Halloween season in the Goth scene starts at least a month in advance, so nightclubbing in late September one invariably encounters a Halloween theme. In 2013, following up on an announcement forthcoming from Sir William Welles, we set out for a bar, Saints and Sinners, situated within a restaurant (Heavenly Bamboo) in Manhattan's Midtown East to attend an event called *City of Dark Angels*. This theme-night took place at various locations every fourth Friday of the month under the auspices of scene personality Archangel Santana. Welles was celebrating the relaunch of his informative directory website New Goth City and chose to host an event called City of Dark Angels at which to promote it.

With Halloween more than a month away, we found the attendees in over-the-top outfits fusing Goth, cyberpunk, and Halloween horror, wearing elaborate wigs, hats, and theatrical makeup. DJs like V Christ, Arch Angel, Paradox, and Erik Aengel manned the turntables.

DJ Aengel has been one of the most sought-after DJs in the greater NYC area and a regular, deejaying at over a hundred parties here in the USA and around the world. He has been at it for over twenty years.

Born in Brooklyn, he started going to music clubs at age fourteen, paid his first visit to the legendary Bank at age sixteen and became completely immersed in the scene, taking on the role of promoter for Hal and Natasha the following year. When the Bank underwent one of its many closures, he transitioned with them to Albion/Batcave at multilevel Downtime, later called Slake. He started guest deejaying in DJ Patrick's room in 2000.

In 2005, he became a resident DJ at Father Jeff's Necromantik, which later became Necropolis. He continued in that role until the Covid lockdown of 2020 brought an end to Windfall, the venue at which it was held.

He was a perennial attendee at Father Sebastiaan's New York edition of the Endless Night Vampire Ball and, in 2005, became a resident DJ for the event until it departed NYC permanently while continuing at major cities in the USA and the world. In 2006, Erik was called upon to deejay at QXT's in Newark, first in Area 51, the heavy-duty industrial space and later the various other rooms, each with its own signature sound.

Erik Aengel's favorites are Goth and darkwave, but his cultural icon is the difficult-to-classify glam rock star David Bowie. His favorite bands are the Dutch dark wavers, Clan of Xymox, electronic groups Empathy Test and Boy Harsher as well as French synth-wavers Carpenter Brut. His best-loved single is "The Spider and the Fly" by London After Midnight. A lover of the arts in general, Erik prefers the high-contrast dark paintings of Caravaggio and the Hammer series of horror films.

At this particular occurrence of City of Dark Angels, above the bar, horror films were shown on a giant screen that would be normally used to project sports events. There was a satisfying mix of techno-industrial as well as classics like Depeche Mode and the Cure. A decent light show and wildly costumed club kids provided eye-candy for our guest from overseas.

We attended another City of Dark Angels a couple of years later, this time held at the lower East Side club Left Field. This theme was Mad Max into the Thunderdome, referencing the Australian motion picture franchise that since 1979 and, in many sequels thereafter, captured and defined the concept of postapocalyptic, meaning the ultraviolent and pieced-together, ragtag appearance of survivors of a civilization-ending catastrophe. That theme plays a minor, peripheral, but definite role in the minds and aesthetic tastes of the Goth subculture. The preceding month the theme had been likewise drawn from postapocalyptic cinema, in that case, *The Crow: City of Angels*. This time the attendees were a who's who of dark event personalities, including, once again, William Welles; Archangel's wife, Gina Divine; and famous bicoastal DJ Ms. Margo, who was there to toast guest DJ Hi-Fi Hillary's birthday. Besides Hillary, regular DJs Erik Aengel and V-Christ were joined by guest DJ Paradox.

Upstairs, there was a performance by an all-female tribute band called Judas Priestess. Downstairs, the dance floor moved to the sound of postpunk eighties and Scandinavian EBM (i.e., Covenant, Apoptygma Berserk, etc.).

Some attendees, in deference to the theme, donned postapocalyptic costumes and makeup, although there was no enforced dress code. Others were attired in basic black. The staff's fantastic wardrobe was assembled and applied by a costume company Post Apocalyptic Warlords and included full-face theatrical makeup; elaborate headdresses; and extensions of metal, rubber, and leather. Host Archangel strolled the place wearing an extra head on an extension above the one he was born with. Chatting with him, we learned that despite his hideous, postapocalyptic appearance, he was deeply commitment to providing a welcoming environment for both newcomers as well as committed denizens of the NYC nightlife scene.

Incantation

A lovely young producer named Xtine (pronounced "Christine"), who had been performing and guest deejaying at underground clubs and adult events since the late 1990s, began cohosting a roving night called Absolution with DJ Jason, of the Limelight and Alchemy fame. Absolution would pop up at odd locations around town, often with little notification outside of the back pages of the Village Voice. The Countess and I made it our business to hunt for these one-off events wherever they were held. Sometimes the venue would be the downstairs at a female impersonators club. Other times the warehouse of a building supply outlet. Once it was in the spacious library of a psychotherapist's office. Attendance was spotty to say the least, and on more than one occasion, the Countess and I were either the only guests or we shared the dance area with only a mere handful of others.

We persevered in seeking and finding events to get our fix of Goth-industrial music and ambience. We didn't expect these nights would be of monumental significance, but one never knew what doors we might be opening. We spent several evenings at Uncle Mike's, a far-downtown bar where DJ Jason and the beautiful blond DJ Xtine were hosting a night they called Incantation. As many as six or seven local as well as visiting bands performed, and Jason spun the best of old and new, classic and obscure Goth and industrial tracks between acts.

One of the best bands to perform at Incantation was our old friend, the combo Ninth House, led by singer-songwriter Mark Sinnis. Goth is a big tent. Once a bouncer at CBGB's Gallery, Mark Sinnis and his band have explored the dark side of country and western to come up with their own unique blend that Mark used to describe as "Johnny Cash meets the Cure."

During my first listen to his band Ninth House, I felt a more appropriate designation was *Cemetery-and-Western*, putting it in the same category as "Ode to Blly Joe" and Willie Nelsons's "Grave Digger." Sinnis's baritonal vocals and pitch-black melodies elevate his music to the highest levels of Goth, albeit blended with folk. Subsequent to Ninth House, he has funneled his musical efforts into a more folksy country and western band called 825, not Goth but with the same heavy sound.

Incantation was much like the many other Goth club nights we had been attending here and there about NYC and seemed unlikely to spark a major turning point in our lives. But it did.

THE WAVE GOTIK TREFFEN

One night in 2012, we attended Incantation at Uncle Mike's, where, as usual, DJ Xtine was spinning. We always enjoyed chatting it up with the young, attractive DJ who was knowledgeable, informative, and friendly. We explained that we were on the eve of a trip to Germany where we had plans with friends who were to meet us there to join us in a tour of the Rhineland. When Xtine heard us mention the trip to Germany, she was astonished that we hadn't made arrangements to include a side trip to the Wave Gotik Treffen, which was taking place while we were in Germany.

Despite our sixteen-year interest in the Goth scene, we had only the most vague notion of the spectacular *Treffen* (German for "meeting" or "convention"), having only heard it mentioned but never explained. Xtine made us to understand that it was the most important conclave of Goths from around the world to celebrate the music and the culture associated with the scene and lifestyle. It turns out to be much more than that!

Quickly modifying our vacation plans, we notified our friends that we would be shortening our stay with them in the Rhineland. We would travel across Germany by train to Leipzig in the east, in the former East Germany, behind the erstwhile Cold War's Iron Curtain. Travel plans were expanded to include this.

Once inside Germany, we boarded a train for Leipzig, satisfied that we had packed enough in the way of black clothing to fit right in with the festival participants. We knew we were on the right train as every stitch of the attire worn by our copassengers was black. Shiny silver jewelry shone on lips, noses, and brows, and in imaginative ways, ears.

We were thoroughly familiar with the couture and accessories from our frequenting the Goth nightclub scene but found it delightful to see them displaying their look out here, in broad daylight, on a train.

We arrived at Leipzig's gargantuan rail station, reputed to be the largest in Europe, and quickly checked into the nearest hotel. Across from the station were kiosks selling tickets to the four-day event and irreversibly crimping a decorative black ribbon wristband that would serve to identify us as paid attendees and permit us to enter the fifty-one venues and myriad events.

The wristbands also granted unlimited access to the city-wide tram system. Maps and schedules were dispensed. For an additional fifteen Euros, we purchased a graphically beautiful, creepily designed and printed hardbound book containing exceptionally beautiful color images, with details about the events, artists, venues, and relevant promotions on glossy (what else?) *black* paper.

Standing in the two-hour line to purchase the requisite wristband granted us the opportunity to observe the fabulously outfitted crowd of participants and attendees lined up for the same purpose. The young woman in front of us in line, though slender, wore a stiff corset and lacy trimmings everywhere—on her shoulder straps, on her elbow-length gloves, on her choker. Everything she wore was, of course, black. In fact, every outfit we observed, with few exceptions, was black. Her arms were wrapped around herself in such a way as to bring her shining black nails, manicured to a menacing point, into view. In contrast to the mainly frilly, feminine attire she wore, her slim legs, scarcely enclosed in the tattered remnants of stockings, were supported within bulky, knee-high, bulbous-toed, thick-soled leather boots. Her male companion, with his temples and the back of his head shaved clean but the thick mop of blackened hair atop his head slicked straight back, wore a shirt with military-styled epaulets and huge, capacious pants, the legs of which issued forth straps with snaps that attached to metal rings installed along the seams.

As we looked around, beautiful and less-than-beautiful girls with androgynous, creative attire meandered about in pairs like harpies drawing attention and admiration. Seated on the grass were a group of young men, one of whom stood out by virtue of his several-inches-high platinum-white pompadour. He was one of several guests who broke the all-black color code. A woman strutted by wearing a huge, billowing white gown of lacy material that might have served as a bridal gown. A bright-red crusader cross stood out on the back of a man wearing a white robe. Ninety-nine percent of the population, however, was in black—black jackets, military dress, or marching-band attire; T-shirts; black pillbox caps, berets, captain's hats, workmen's caps (some of these in olive drab); tights, fishnet stockings, or shirts; and Victorian mourning outfits. In addition to the vampire look of capes, amulets, and fangs, there were those wearing steampunk style, which included top hats, crinoline dresses, corsets, parasols, and walking sticks.

Oh, and the mohawks! The mohawks hairdos on display exceeded anything we had observed in the States in terms of height, coloration, and grooming at WGT. The tresses of those in attendance appeared in colors rarely seen in nature, such as intense pink, aqua-turquoise, and hot orange, whether groomed into mohawks or less lofty hairdos.

The crowd consisted mainly of young adults, but there were elderlies and families with children as well. Some infants were propped up in little black carriages or strollers, pushed dutifully by parents in Edwardian attire and accompanied by toddler and preteen siblings. On a street corner, a muscular young man tightened the laces on his female companion's corset. Someone in a Guy Fawkes mask and a butcher's apron was seen leaning comfortably against a wall. Three black-clad young men walked side by side, engaged in animated conversation. One of whom had smeared bright-red theatrical blood from the top of his shaved head down half his face. A couple of British punks were seen sitting at an outdoor bar. The pants of one and the shoes of the other bore the recognizable colors and patterns of the Union Jack.

The city's tram system made it feasible to hop from live performances to DJ parties, to church-choir events, to cinema, to lectures, and to art exhibitions (many of which were in English). On the first night, at the huge, hangar-like convention center called Agra, we attended performances by German industrial band Eisbrecher that had a Laibach-like, militaristic sound and the group Tanzwut, featuring bagpipe accompaniment. Idols of the Dutch dark wave Clan of Xymox and electro-industrialists Project Pitchfork added variety, while all around Leipzig, in clubs, dance halls, concert spaces and bars, numerous other musical performances were going on at the same time and would continue doing so for the next three days.

Agra also contains a huge shopping mall where items of clothing, costumes, fetish accessories, footwear, helmets, headdresses, and the like are for sale. One of the great delights of the festival is to stroll through this section browsing and occasionally succumbing to make purchases of unique items. It also contains an ongoing exhibition featuring grotesque works of explicit art.

As an indication of the breadth and depth of the WGT experience, the festival included access to the Art Museum Der Bildenden Künste where Dutch masters and modern art are on display; to organ concerts at the church where Johann Sebastian Bach performed and is presently entombed; to the Leipzig Opera House; a picturesque bar featuring a menu of three hundred absinthe drinks; and to the oldest, continuously operating restaurant in Europe, the devil-themed Auerbachs Keller where Goethe was inspired to write the play "Faust."

At the end of three days of round-the-clock immersion in the deep depths of this all-Goth-all-the-time festival, we were left dizzy with questions about the meaning of it all. One of the last sights we saw before surfacing back into the bright and sunny world of everyday life, was a young man wearing a black shirt with an inscription that seemed to sum it all up: "Dunkel Schön," which translates to "Dark is beautiful."

In the decade that followed, the Countess and I visited Leipzig several more times, and we learned that the Wave Gotik Treffen is much more than that. Just as the annual festival of Wave Gotik Treffen in Leipzig, Germany, owes its existence to the emergence of the Goth subculture, so too the Goth subculture owes as much to that festival, which, in a sense, sustains it. And that is because Wave Gotik Treffen is the very apotheosis of Goth. Goth is a concept, and WGT is its embodiment, crystallized into flesh-and-blood, mortar-and-concrete form.

History of WGT

Sprung from the cultural ferment at the end of the Cold War and the emergence of pent-up desire for free expression upon the collapse of the Soviet Union's hold on East Germany, WGT emerged in 1991. In the years preceding the first WGT, Germany was divided into two nation-states: a Communist police state in the East and a free democracy in the West. There existed a sharp demarcation both politically and culturally between the two sides of the border. In the mid-to-late 1980s, the Cure conducted several tours of the free Western-allied West Germany, whetting the appetite of East German youth on the other side of the border for the modern music and the style that they represented. By 1985, youth within the oppressed Eastern sector were imitating the postpunk look and appearance of Robert Smith and passing around bootleg tapes of the Cure.

They grew increasingly frustrated, knowing that bands like the Cure and Depeche Mode were touring in West Germany. Their early attempt to stage a WGT, in 1987, got crushed by the Communist authorities. Then the Berlin Wall fell in 1989, and Germany was soon reunited. In commemoration, there is a museum dedicated to examining the evil deeds of the East German Secret Police, the *Stasi,* which be discussed below.

The first real WGT took place in Leipzig in1991 and began recurring every year, every spring, growing bigger and managed better each time. Wave Gotik Treffen recurs annually on the weekend preceding the church holiday of *Pfingsten* (i.e., Pentecost Monday), which is a national holiday in Germany, allowing for a three-day-weekend festival.

Goth enthusiasts from around the world come each year to exchange styles of music, fashion, appearance, and cultural practices. And each year they return to their home countries carrying back the newest and latest trends that will become components of the Goth scene and lifestyle that integrate into their existing social settings.

In that way, WGT is like a recurring big bang that spreads and fertilizes the worldwide Goth scene. When attendees from around the world gather back the following year, they cross-fertilize the scene with fresh elements that will redistribute across the globe following the Treffen.

What Goes on at WGT

Oil on canvas painting, Between sets at WGT

Morizbastei is a huge stone building that historically served as an armory, defense fortification, and jail. Now it houses multiple bars, restaurants, and dance rooms. NYC's own top DJ, Sean Templar, mans the booth, spinning his signature "When We Were Young" mix.

One may cruise the upper deck of Moritzbastei where vendors display handcrafted (as well as "made in China") dark-themed artworks, garments, and accessories. A variety of tasty alcoholic and nonalcoholic drinks are served. Usually, a group of musicians in medieval costumes—horned helmets, furs, feather headdresses—play traditional instruments (bagpipes, fiddles, and the like), evoking images of the real, original Goths of ancient Europe.

For the twenty-fifth anniversary in 2016, the Museum of the City of Leipzig put on an exhibition called Leipzig in Schwarz (Leipzig in Black) where photos, explanatory posters, models, record jackets, sculptures, and installation artworks were on display, documenting the Gothic subculture that had spawned the annual Wave Gotik Treffen and tracing its growth into the massive and complex phenomenon that is today. A commemorative hardcover book with an introduction by Goth luminary Andi Harriman was available for sale at the museum.

Agra is the giant indoor fairgrounds, large enough to accommodate any crowd, where most of the headliners appear. Half of this cavernous hall is given over to a vast and diverse marketplace for vendors of everything from costumes, garments, and jewelry to accoutrements and accessories like helmets, goggles, gas masks, and fetish attire. There, one might stop at the booth of famous Father Sebastiaan to schedule an appointment to have real, wearable fangs fabricated by the fang master.

In addition to musical events, one can visit Leipzig's many museums. Unique among which is the museum dedicated to collecting and categorizing the massive store of surviving records from the former East German Communist spy agency, the *Stasi* (a compression of the German words for state security), where English-language guided tours and lectures are conducted. For the WGT festival, the emphasis is on the Stasi's ludicrous obsession with spying, infiltrating, and studying the curious subcultures that were springing up in the 1980s, namely, Goths (whom they called Gruftis), punks, and heavy metalheads. File cards on teenage alternative music fans are displayed and explained, mug shots of kids who were dolled up like Robert Smith of the Cure hung from the agency walls, and room upon room containing hundreds of thousands of paper files (said to measure up to five miles in height if stacked) are shown.

There are also Egyptian art and historic museums as well as numerous galleries and shops that take up the Gothic theme for the festival, whether it is a prominent anniversary year or not.

One could always take a break at the Absintherie Sixtina, a bar whose menu boasts no less than 237 varieties of absinth plus dozens of cocktails above and beyond beer and wine. There was a tent-covered outdoors garden with its own little service bar in back, and it was furnished with picnic tables. Indoors there was ongoing a series of band performances. One could find oneself seated in tight confines in a booth with some interesting and, I might add, beautiful festivalgoers from places as far away as Greenland!

Late night was best spent sampling various DJs in one of the several dance halls at Moritzbastei. In the morning, one might return there to eat at the cafeteria and tour the art exhibition posted on the walls and halls of the building.

A stop at the Heathen Village (a.k.a. Pagan Village) provided live music from a stage and a picnic-like outdoor experience, a sort of Ren-Faire, which serves as a reminder of the historical Goths of the Middle Ages in Europe but filled with modern-day and postmodern Goths in black. At this twenty-fifth anniversary iteration of WGT, New York's own Aurelio Voltaire performed his original, antifolk music and stand-up act, chiding his audience with good-natured barbs.

Free access was available to Leipzig's Grand Opera House and to a theater across town where, this year (2016), there was a live performance of the musical *Dracula*. When these theaters run out of free passes, one can still purchase affordable tickets to the featured performances.

Wave Gotik Treffen serves to distill the very essence of Goth. By bringing together Goths from all around the world, it expands and renews world Goth culture, incorporating novel takes on the various themes of music, glamour, art, and style.

OTHER MAJOR AND RECURRING EVENTS

No gathering or festival can top the size, extent, and attendance of Germany's Wave Gotik Treffen, which takes over much of the city of Leipzig and draws many thousands from around the world. Nevertheless, Greater NYC provides several extravagant events that, in their own way, rival WGT in scope, if not size or duration.

Dark Side of the Con

For three consecutive years, 2017, 2018, and 2019, Jet Berelson's online community, Vampire Freaks, hosted a major three-day convention, featuring everything dark and creepy, whether musical or fashion related. A lot of it had a sly, tongue-in-cheek aspect. Dark Side of the Con was billed as "North America's Dark-Alternative Convention." It was held at various New Jersey hotels, demonstrating that Goth culture was not merely the wearing of black clothes but a broad cultural phenomenon, including music, art, history, and the sociology of Goth culture. Even a lecture and demonstration of live bats was presented by a state-licensed wildlife exhibitor. Dark Side was exactly the kind of affair that the Countess and I could be counted upon to attend.

Featured were many bands, live and onstage, some internationally recognized; DJs of great renown within the postpunk, electronic, and industrial fields; late-night dance parties; costume contests; naughty burlesque shows; and live reenactment of classic cinema. Panels, workshops, and lectures abounded on such subjects as the paranormal, rope bondage, horror literature, mask making, and elders of Goth.

Famous club nights like Stimulate, QXT's, Cybertron, and the Red Party transplanted their DJs, much of their ambience and many of their loyal following to dedicated rooms for dance events. We roamed the hotel's halls and corridors, lined at all times with vendors selling artworks, jewelry, garments, accessories, literature, and more. The greatest joy may have come from sighting stunningly glamorous attendees, some scantily clad and others decidedly overdressed, strolling the halls. My comanager from Empire Hideous days, Mr. Haunt, brought his kids to be entertained in a salon that offered spooky storytelling, coloring, and painting. I participated as a panelist at a discussion of "Elder Goths."

With Mr. Haunt's voluntary assistance and that of famous diesel punk artist Charlie Garlette, I was able to set up a booth for display of my artwork. For the preceding several years, I had worked on producing a series of portrait paintings on canvas, some in oil and some in acrylic, featuring Goth icons. These ran the gamut from Bela Lugosi to Bettie Page and included such literary notables as writer Mary Shelley and philosopher Friedrich Nietzsche and, of course, Goth rock giants such as Peter Murphy, Mike Ness, and Siouxsie Sioux. Many originals as well as prints were sold to a diverse group of supporters of the arts. The final purchase, a portrait of the Cure's Robert Smith, was made by Jet VF himself.

Every iteration of Dark Side of the Con concluded with satisfying feelings, happiness, and a sense of belonging to a community. While operations were suspended during 2020, plans were announced to reincarnate the event as Dark Force Fest in 2023.

The man behind Dark Side is one of the top producers of postpunk events in the greater NYC area: *Jet Berelson*, or *Jet VF* (for *V*ampire *F*reaks). He is the impresario behind numerous top-flight events, performances, shows and the organizer of the erstwhile online community, now a merchandise store, catering to the Goth scene. Jet grew up in a neighborhood in Brooklyn that he describes as rife with crime, and where he endured constant harassment. He describes himself as "just a dorky kid and dealing with depression" during childhood and adolescence.

MTV was his entry portal to, first, mainstream popular music, then such cutting-edge bands as Nine Inch Nails and Marilyn Manson. Something caused him to relate to the darker aesthetic; perhaps the morose view on life that he had acquired growing up. Already feeling alienated, he dove further into Goth/industrial music, discovering bands like the Cure, KMFDM, Skinny Puppy, Ministry, and Siouxsie and the Banshees.

Jet admits to using a fake ID in order to get into to the NYC postpunk clubs at age sixteen where he made friends and became a regular attendee at local Goth events. He knew he had found his home.

Attending the University of Rochester, he received a degree in computer science. In 1999, he started the website VampireFreaks.com, which started out as personal website, to test out his website programming skills. It included some pictures of his friends and a message board that grew in popularity.

The Vampire Freaks website created an opportunity to establish an online clothing store specializing in Gothic style attire. In 2004, he created the Vampire Freaks social network site, which grew to be the largest Goth website in the world, with millions of members worldwide while thriving before the pandemic lockdown.

Through Vampire Freaks, Jet hosted a variety of concerts and club nights in NYC since 2000, such as the Cybertron NYC club night, the Triton Festival, and, of course, Dark Side of the Con, which is North America's largest Goth convention.

Vampire Freaks stopped being a social networking site in early 2020 to focus on its ecommerce and event promotions, and since then has been growing in size as a leading dark alternative clothing site, now operating out of a four-thousand-square-foot warehouse with a team of full-time employees.

A Murder of Crows

This two day-and-night summer festival takes its name from the colorful collective noun used to denote a flock, or gathering of crows. We attended the 2018 entry of this recurring annual event. It was held like most in the series at Brooklyn Bazaar in mid-September of that year.

When we attended, our interest was first captivated at the dark market merchandise space at the ground level where merchants presented wickedly themed and crafted curiosities and advocacy-group manned booths giving voice to their respective causes. DJs worked both the upstairs performance hall between live sets and the basement-level after-hours dance room. After making nominal purchases in support of the artists, we attended the live performances upstairs. Musical groups came from all around the country, their styles ranging from bombastic to Western twangy guitars, all more or less morose and dark.

When we had satisfied our interest in experiencing live performances by some bands that were new to us, we dropped to the basement level for the nightclub disco dance party where famous DJs Dave Bats, Martin Oldgoth, Patrick, and Sean Templar himself served up the finest selection of postpunk, new wave, and deathrock.

The Endless Night Vampire Ball

With the Countess's growing interest and enthusiasm, I looked for opportunities to explore all the various tributaries of the Goth subculture. Because of the demands of both our professional lives, we made only occasional stops at weekly dance clubs, preferring to limit our weekend (and occasional weekday) sojourns to more major events like the annual Anti-Valentines Balls held at various venues each year. These were hosted by the most internationally successful impresario, Father Sebastiaan. He made his start sponsoring Long Black Veil club nights back in the early 1990s and ended up kind of high priest of a worldwide vampire-oriented community. Once a dental technician, he became famous for fabricating custom, wearable fangs under the brand name Sabretooth. Father Sebastiaan combined that activity with producing his own unique series of multiple entertainment event called Endless Night Vampire Balls. These featured live bands, costumed dancers, striptease acts, and costume contests.

Endless Night Vampire Ball

Father Sebastiaan had been one of the earliest and most prominent creators within the NYC Goth scene to publicly recognize me and celebrate my presence at his events, which undoubtedly expanded and deepened my commitment to the scene. These Vampire Ball events originated as Long Black Veil club nights in the Meatpacking district during the 1990s, eventually becoming worldwide Sabertooth and Endless Night events run by Father Sebastiaan and Victor Magnus with locations in New Orleans; Los Angeles; Paris; Amsterdam; Dallas; London; and Tampa, Florida.

Endless Night Vampire Balls had their inception in 1998 and were not limited to anti-Valentines events, but occurred at appropriate intervals throughout the year. These were held at various venues: Club True, Rare, the Bank, and Drom. The most fitting of all was the uptown Jekyll and Hyde restaurant/club in NYC's theater district. There, the slick and creepy animated installations and the costumed staff and live actors provided a perfect run-up to the ball itself held in a dungeon-like chamber with eerie props abounding. There, we got to see a gentleman convincingly costumed as Vlad the Impaler; a pair of shapely, marauding, vampire bat sisters costumed like Egyptian deities; as well as myriad Victorian and Edwardian villains. And we got to hear soprano Ariel De Ment powerfully belt out an aria from the opera *Carmen*. Goth taste in music stretches, we came to learn, to include classical! Endless Night Balls eventually expanded into major extravaganzas at locations around the world. The most noteworthy of these recurred on Halloween in New Orleans, Louisiana, where we flew several times to find the whole city in a frenzy of ghastly events layered onto the already voodoo-themed, otherworldly culture of the town.

Staying at a hotel on Canal Street provided easy access to the fabulous attractions in the French Quarter, where Halloween celebrations abounded. First up was the Ghost and Vampire Tour conducted by the highly informative and eccentric character Lord Chaz in top hat and six-inch platform shoes that lifted his barrel-shaped body to a lofty and intimidating six feet six inches. We were summoned with up to forty fellow tourists to gather at a dive bar, Johnny White's Hole in the Wall, where the tour began.

We were led on an hour-and-a-half walk through the French Quarter while Chaz told us tales of mass murders, unsolved mysteries, and reports of apparition sightings. He spent particular time and detail in narrating a series of unconfirmed reports against a convent where remains of buried infants were allegedly found.

Chaz spices up his presentation with autobiographical assertions of his own otherworldliness, starting with his ability to stop his own heart. Indeed, several doctors and nurses on the tour confirmed that he was able to interrupt the pulse at his wrists at will. He also allowed those on the tour to touch his skin in order to confirm his claim to have a body surface temperature like that of a cold cadaver, despite wearing layers of robes and a hat over his long, shoulder-length hair. Indeed, I have touched many cadavers in my capacity as a medical student and a doctor, and Lord Chaz's flesh felt every bit as dead. Finally, at the conclusion of the tour, he performed a trick display of opening a bleeding wound in his forearm with one of his inch-and-a-half pointed fingernails, drinking what seemed to be blood from it, then displaying a clean, intact forearm where the wound had been. We were left aghast and astonished at these gruesome displays that ended the tour and ready to take in the rest of Halloween in NOLA.

Next we attended the Lestat Coronation Ball, the main social event of the Anne Rice Vampire Lestat Fan Club, held during a convention called the Undead Con. Anne Rice, Her Gray Eminence, viewed and addressed the crowd from a balcony on high, like the pope of a devout but mischievous congregation. Although not readers of Anne Rice's vampire novels, we felt sufficient camaraderie to stay for a few songs sung live by Mary Fahl, who had written a song, "Exiles," for the audiobook version of Rice's novel *The Wolves of Midwinter*. I had always suspected that Mary Fahl, whom I recalled as the vocalist of the midnineties Montclair, New Jersey, based folk-rock band October Project and who looks and sounds every bit the part of an angel, drew inspiration from a deep well of darkness; and her presence as a headliner here proved it.

The Endless Night Anti-Valentine Halloween Vampire Ball was, of course, the highlight of the trip. It took place at the retro-atmospheric NOLA House of Blues and proved to be one of the most over-the-top entertaining and social events ever to arise from this eccentric and eclectic subculture. Goths, self-identifying vampires, full-time dwellers of the underground, as well as poseur wannabes were treated to a true spectacular of music and performance art concocted by Father Sebastiaan and his crew of assistants, artists, performers, DJs, and technicians. The theme was Victoriental, and the crowd was gorgeously attired and costumed in Victorian, Baroque, vampirish, glamorous, and horrific costumes.

Heavy EBM and Goth rock filled the air and the dance floor was in endless motion. Young and not-so-young mingled affably and the mood was celebratory almost to the point of being giddy. Wandering the House of Blues we found an upstairs side room where a somewhat tame ritual was taking place. Downstairs, a French-accented, flamboyant, and baroque-attired emcee came on stage and announced the first entertainment of the night. Multitalented soprano Ariel De Ment came on stage and belted out, first, an opera aria and then the heartrending "Point of No Return" from the *Phantom of the Opera*.

A belly dancer followed accompanied by a kilt-clad violinist playing Middle Eastern and Celtic melodies. After that came a burlesque dancer followed by a staged metaphysical vampire ritual involving swordplay, bullwhip cracking, a priestess, and several scantily clad acolytes. The headline band was Metropolis Records artist

Bella Morte, who performed an hour-long set of melodious metal rock. Eventually, Father Sebastiaan came onstage to oversee the selection of the winner of the costume contest. The prize went to a young woman wearing something like a wedding gown, perhaps a reference to some horror movie or persona of whom I'm unaware. DJs played darkwave/dance during the intervals between acts and following the last act. The party went on into the early morning hours.

St. Louis Cemetery

Halloween is All Saint's Eve, so the following day we went on a tour of a cemetery, again, with Lord Chaz. St. Louis Cemetery No.1 is the oldest still-operating cemetery in New Orleans. Like almost all cemeteries in that part of the world, it features aboveground tombs. Some famous names are here. None is more notorious than the tomb with the remains of voodoo priestess Marie Laveau (1801?–1881?). So it didn't surprise us to see a picturesque young woman with orange pigtails kneeling in front of the Creole voodoo queen's tomb to perform a ritual for All Saint's Day with candles, icons, tobacco smoke, and an alcoholic beverage. The doorstep to the tomb was overflowing with floral bouquets and an indescribable offering of three or four ovals of plant flesh on a platter, each a different shade of brown. It's a tableau, an image, that's hard to forget.

The Last Endless Night Vampire Ball in NYC

In 2016, we attended a spectacular NYC occurrence of Father Sebastiaan's Endless Night Vampire Ball at Slake, a multilevel club on the site of what used to be the Albion/Batcave at Downtime. Gatekeeper Victor Magnus greeted guests and stamped Sabretooth's emblematic ankh on each ticketholder's wrist. We were directed upstairs, where we were accosted in a friendly manner by a suave gent who offered and carried through with his offer to give couples dance lessons in how to waltz. We and a few other couples took that lesson, but sooner or later the three-fourths waltz timing was replaced by the more standard four-fourths rock music beat as strains of the Sisters of Mercy came to fill the air.

As on all Endless Night Vampire balls, Father Sebastiaan appeared on stage to welcome the crowd. He then called for remembrance of those of his "clan," who had passed from the scene and led the crowd in a ritual howl as was the tradition at all such gatherings seemingly a reference to the kinship between vampires and (were) wolves.

The entertainment was ghastly-themed, mildly raunchy, and always captivating. Starting off there were a pair of scantily, all-white-clad, Baroque-styled and wigged dancers who put on a stylized, tasteful, not-too-explicit R-rated ballet referring to a 1724 pamphlet titled "The Heinous Sin of Self-Pollution," decrying the practice of onanism.

After several years of recurrences, impresario and fang master Father Sebastiaan staged the final NYC Vampire Ball at Drom on the Lower East Side's Avenue A on October 20, 2018. The series continues at various cultural capitals of the world.

Gothcon 2001

A national convention of all things Gothic (actually the second occurrence of the event) was held in March 2001 in America's capital for deviant, counterculture, the "Big Easy," New Orleans, Louisiana (NOLA). The meeting included everything from band performances, costume contests, and magic shows to panel discussions, independent films, and poetry readings. We stayed nearby in The Crescent, a seedy hotel if ever there was one, which boasted dingy hallways, peeling paint, mildewed bathrooms, missing light bulbs, and ice-cold rooms with paper-thin walls that transmitted every sound into the adjoining rooms.

Goths of every stripe, transgressives of every deviant inclination—industrial freaks, punks, multipierced, tattooed, mohawk-tressed, transgendered, vampiric, and fetishistic—promenaded throughout the three days in black attire ranging from merely basic black to unimaginably flamboyant makeup and costumes. Each day of staged musical groups and events in the main ballroom was topped off with a night of dance featuring various DJs. Another room provided a venue for readings and discussion groups such as "Being Goth in the Corporate World" and "Bondage 101," sponsored by the National Coalition for Sexual Freedom and panel discussions for musicians, would-be DJs, promoters, and filmmakers. Optional tours of the city included stops in front of the homes of two Goth icons: author Anne Rice and Nine Inch Nails' Trent Reznor.

NY/NJ's own artistic community's short-lived organization The Rift moderated by the fashionably attired and erudite Madame X, hosted events for writers of dark prose and poetry. Cinematographer Joe Christ upheld his self-confessed reputation for nauseatingly offensive and pointlessly revolting, bottom-of-the-barrel quality home movies that could only appeal to the depraved.

The band performances ranged from pathetic, wedding-band style music, through the mediocre, to the memorable Gothic-industrial band The Last Dance. The high point in the festival occurred the last night with a performance by Aurelio Voltaire, who used to go by the monomer "Voltaire," a prolific songwriter raconteur, graphic novelist, video animator, and acid social critic. Earlier in the convention, he had served as a discussant on panels covering various topics of interest to the Goth community and had used his sarcastic wisdom to head off any tendency of the audience or other speakers to take themselves or their issues too seriously. Long recognized as the leading, multitalented contributor to the NYC Goth scene, he was noted at this convention to have a nationwide following as well.

Self-accompanying on acoustic guitar, Voltaire practically brought the house down with his antifolk style; ingenious, irreverent lyrics; catchy melodies; and acerbic wit, distinguishing himself from all stereotypes held of Gothcon 2001.

Dracula's Ball

Patrick Rodgers Opening Address At Dracula's Ball

In September of 2001, I attended my first Dracula's Ball with the Countess. Dracula's Ball is a unique, dress-up musical event that rotated four times a year at various venues in Philadelphia. On this occurrence, and many occasions thereafter, it was held at the Trocadero, a beautifully refurbished nineteenth-century vaudeville and burlesque house. There was a lobby space called the rialto for vendors of clothes, unearthly crafts, gloomy artwork, ghoulish accessories, depressing décor, and, of course, Vampire-brand condoms. This provided a perfect space for just milling about, taking in the sights of Goths in ghastly costumes or formal wear.

There was no dress code, but we didn't see any attendees in jeans, sneakers, business clothes, or colorful sports attire. Instead, there were extravagantly appointed outfits in medieval, priestly, and Victorian attire in regular fabrics or latex, leather, mesh, and lingerie as outerwear.

Once inside, we entered a semicircular atrium that embraced a sunken dance floor that was a few steps down. Beyond it was a large theater-size stage. Dark danceable music filled the air, and many patrons were dancing in the characteristic smooth gyrating style that we recognized from the club scene in NYC and NJ. Some of the music was recognizably that of the Sisters of Mercy and the Cruxshadows, but much of it was curated by DJ Schmitty, who spun mainly the variety of unrecognizable techno-industrial that is without vocals.

Patrick Rodgers, the brains behind the record company, Dancing Ferret, a tall goateed figure in a long black leather overcoat, came on stage and made welcoming comments through an elaborate set of permanently implanted fangs. He announced the entertainment bill for the night that would commence with an Ohio-based darkwave band called Thou Shall Not. The headliners, that would come on very late after several more opening bands, were international electronic superstars Neuroticfish, from Germany. Sixteen or seventeen years later, I was to again see this group live at the Wave Gotik Treffen, about which much was said earlier. Festivities (i.e., dancing) at this and future Dracula's Balls typically went on into the early morning hours.

The Countess and I would go on to attend countless iterations of Dracula's Ball, including spectacular Halloween special events, many at the now defunct Shampoo nightclub where three or more dance floors were provided, even including an outdoor space where die-hard cigarette addicts were banished in compliance with Philadelphia's indoor venue regulations.

It was not uncommon to encounter members of the NYC and North Jersey Goth community, notably scene-activist Madame X, and to hear internationally famous Goth bands like Project Pitchfork. In its heyday, Dracula's Ball was the significant Goth event in the tristate region taking in New York, New Jersey, and Pennsylvania.

CASTLE PARTY

Castle Party

One of the most satisfying and affirming experiences is to unexpectedly come across evidence of a group of previously unknown fellow travelers on the life's journey, people who you didn't realize shared your opinions or ideals, or even aesthetic taste. So when a young Polish lady with whom we chanced to have a passing conversation recommended that on our next trip to Europe we should spend three days at the annual Castle Party in Poland, we had no clear idea of what to expect.

Palac(e) Jastrowiec

Researching the event, we learned that it was to be held in a remote region of Poland, accessible mainly by car over small country roads. Fortunately, we were able to start this trek from Warsaw, where lived two loyal friends, willing and able to transport us to our destination. They drove us halfway across the country to the extreme southwest corner by the Czech border in what once was a German-speaking region called Lower Silesia. Once we reached the nearest city, Wroclaw (pronounced "Fro-swav"), the erstwhile German city of Breslow, we still had over an hour of driving to our first destination, an eighteenth-century palace owned (until the end of World War II) by the Hoyos-Sprizenstein family.

We found the Palace Jastrowiec to be a stately, three-storey, crumbling baroque chateau surrounded by a dry moat and run as an *agrotourism* hotel by an elderly couple who reside in Berlin during the off-season. Its central atrium is surmounted by a glass skylight in subdued colors of blue and rose. Dark winding staircases light up with motion detection. There are many fireplaces; a dining hall where meals are served; and several grand drawing rooms, libraries, and parlors (one featuring a piano that has not been tuned in the better part of a century). Solemn oil paintings adorned the walls.

Our hostess was a somber, well-mannered, solicitous matron who spoke German and Polish. She led us to our room. We passed through several locked passageways to arrive at our accommodation—a bright, capacious room with a redundancy of beds and sofas—and were given the necessary keys. She would arrange, we learned, to recruit a local boy to drive us at any hours of the day and night to and from the castle where the festival was to begin on the outskirts of the nearby town of Bolkow the next morning.

We took a late breakfast the next morning. Then we dressed up in all black and stepped outside, where an affable young man, Tomek, was waiting to drive us in his tiny European automobile. After a ten-minute ride, we entered Bolkow, a village of about five thousand local inhabitants, now overrun with black-clad Goths. Rows of tightly aligned masonry buildings faced the broad main drag. There were few local pedestrians or moving vehicles. Housewives, some with small children, gazed out from stoops and porches. We came to a church in front of which stood a statue of John Paul II, the late Polish pope, his arms outstretched in benediction over a crowd of black-clad Goths milling about. Tomek stopped the car and let us out at the foot of a cobblestone-paved street that led up a steep hill toward the castle.

Making sure we had Tomek's phone for summoning a return ride later in the day, we disembarked and began the trudge up the street. On either side, there were stands with food, beer, costumes, souvenirs, and handcrafted brass and copper jewelry, rings and necklace items, including bird and bat heads, amulets, and, of course, skulls. A couple of bakers dressed as monks tended an oven where they were preparing flat bread and, I think, cheese: a rustic Polish version of pizza. At the first plateau of the hill was a food truck with awnings and banners declaring the brands of beer sold: Zwiec and Grolsch.

At that point, we turned to face the path, still cobblestoned, leading up to the castle. It was still daylight. Looking upward, we could see the tall rectangular gray brick tower with an enormous banner emblazoned with the words "Castle Party," the two words separated by a silhouetted figure of a knight galloping on horseback holding a mace or battle-ax aloft. Both the tower and the surrounding defensive wall were topped with medieval architectural crenelations, the notches that space the blocks apart, creating a sort of crown atop the roof. In the spaces between the blocks, medieval archers would have been afforded partial protection while shooting arrows down on invaders below.

The path up to it was steep and still arranged into cobblestone steps. We joyfully joined the parade marching upward like we were climbing a stairway to heaven. We arrived at a lesser tower situated at the edge of the plateau from which the castle arose. There, officials collected our payments and applied our identifying wristbands. We then passed through a stone archway to a vast field of trodden grass, where a crowd was beginning to gather.

Costumes as imaginative and bizarre as any we had seen at Dracula's Ball in Philadelphia were everywhere. Victorian garb, barbarian outfits, metal, leather, and fur were in evidence. Extraordinary varieties of footwear: shoes with heels, high and low boots (industrial, military, and fetishistic including thigh-high, knee-high, and ankle-high), stockings (sheer and fishnets, and some designs that we had never seen before). A few wore giant headdresses, some in the form of skulls: human and animal. Other's headgear, tribal or futuristic, appeared bobbing above the crowd. Black-clad, eye-poppingly beautiful women made up to resemble vampires smiled, pleased to allow photographers to take their pictures. Here and there, Slavic giants up to seven feet tall were seen towering above the crowd, casual and comfortable in their flat-soled shoes.

The stage, situated at the far end of the field, came alive with activity. As the members of the thrash metal band Kat (Polish for "executioner") took their positions, the PA system pumped out a few bars of "Night on Bald Mountain" as a prelude to the band. Then gravel-voiced Roman Kostrzewski, charged out to center stage, his white mane flowing behind, roaring harshly, to a pounding beat and squealing guitars. The audience came alive with headbangers gyrating and bouncing for the better part of an hour, eventually exhausted at the end of the set.

Following Kat came a mournful Swiss band, aptly named Lacrimosa, with elaborate instrumentation that included guitars, accordion, synthesizers, and symphonic strings to accompany alternating male and female vocalists. Their sound was intriguing, with touches of heavy metal, classical, Central European folk, and even early twentieth-century cabaret, creating an aura of timelessness that transcended rock music.

On our first and on every subsequent visit to Castle Party, we found it absolutely mandatory to visit the small stage venue called Former Evangelical Church, a gutted out, previous chapel that had served the largely Lutheran congregation when the region was inhabited by Germans prior to the end of World War II. It transformed into a setting for smaller, mostly local bands, which concentrated on indie and experimental groups. There we listened to dark, symphonic music. We also watched grainy black-and-white videos of church and cemetery ruins set to noise tracks, and we saw various forms of performance art including "music" made with a metal grinder. In later years, the former Evangelical church was finally abandoned and replaced by Bolkow's town meeting hall for the same purposes.

Again and again, we were treated to distinctive rock music with Slavic, Germanic, and Celtic elements. To a far greater extent than American youth, Europeans remain in contact with historical-cultural roots, blending older traditions into modern rock. This was observed on each of the three times we attended Castle Party in Bolkow. Once, this tendency seemed to go over the top, with the theatrical ensemble Corvus Corax, a group costumed as wild men in masks and kilts who blasted tribal and medieval anthems on bagpipes, drums, rattles, and noisemakers, almost a parody of a Ren Faire sideshow. Whether intended as a spoof or not, it was a fun performance and appeared to have avid fans who took them quite seriously.

Of the many scores of shows we attended over the years at Castle Party, one performance set forth a particularly gloomy future. The multimedia Austrian trio NEO (acronym for Near Earth Objects) performed electronic tracks accompanying computerized videos that portrayed, in clearly understood detail, every possible cataclysm that could befall the modern world from technology and ecology run amok: stray asteroids that might collide with Earth, artificial intelligence turned sinister, computer viruses, alien invasions, treacherous machines, pandemics, nuclear disasters, weaponized drones, and industrial accidents.

We recognized it to be the kind of apocalyptic prophecy that not only sows gloom but also serves to justify the prevailing attitude of alienation from today's world within the Goth-industrial scene. I once attended an all-industrial Monsters of Rock show in NYC and heard a front man take the microphone to announce, gloatingly, that the radioactive waste from the Fukushima nuclear disaster was now spreading worldwide across the planet's oceans and was already contaminating the West Coast harbors of the United States. This suggested a kind of smug "look at the world you've left us" critique that fuels some of the rebelliousness underlying the nonconformity of the Goth scene. It can also be understood as a Nietzschean embrace of adversity rather than running from it.

Many outside the Goth-industrial community look with disapproval, even revulsion, at this seemingly cynical, even nihilistic, embrace of negativity. But the Goth-industrial focus is to draw strength from confronting the negative with unflinching acceptance.

STEAMPUNK EVENT(S)

Chronologie: The Steampunk Event

Steampunk as a style had been knocking around for a few years, but I didn't identify with it until after 2010. An event called Chronologie, created by recognized Goth promoter Sir William Wells, took place at an upscale restaurant Lillie's on Times Square. The place itself had a refined Victorian feel owing to the antique décor and layout. For a few months in 2012 and 2013, the drinking, dining, and listening event Chronologie took place on the first Saturday of each month.

The style termed steampunk derives from multiple antecedent sources, most especially the fiction of H. G. Wells, Jules Verne, and Mary Shelley, in which the early technology of the eighteenth and nineteenth centuries are envisioned as contraptions capable of spectacular achievements like space flight, laser weaponry, etc. Enthusiasm for steampunk included very individualized costumes referring to Victorian styles and adventure fiction of the 1800s and early 1900s.

In keeping with the overall retro-futuristic theme, absinthe (the "Green Fairy") was the favored beverage at Chronologie events, although not by all attendees who imbibed. Only legalized in the USA in 2007, it had the allure of a forbidden commodity, to say nothing of its false reputation for being a mild hallucinogen. At Chronologie, it mainly served as a statement of harkening back to the Age of Steam, of European *fin de siècle* poets, painters, and café society.

Edwardian-attired nostalgia buffs and New Romantics might groove to Fred Astaire's "Putting on the Ritz" or an electro-swing version of "Dance of the Sugar Plum Fairies." The minor-key, banjo-and-fiddle-driven syncopated folk style of steampunk musical icons Abney Park most closely fit the musical sense of the evening.

The "civilian" Times Square tourist types gawked at anachronistically attired, top-hatted, goggled-scene insiders, largely a mix of actors, actresses, promoters, artists, literary types, and Goth-scene crossovers. Whenever celebrity personality Aurelio Voltaire made a cameo appearance, he would become the center of attention for photo-taking Japanese tourists. Although those in attendance seemed to be having the time of their life, the recurring-event Chronologie eventually fizzled out of existence after just a few more recurrences.

A Steampunk Vampire Ball

In 2011, impresario Father Sebastiaan modified the Annual Halloween Endless Night Vampire Ball into a steampunk soiree. It was held on the nearest Saturday to Halloween at the House of Blues in New Orleans, and the Countess and I were determined to attend despite our inflexible Monday-through-Friday work schedules. So we flew down after work on Friday, checked into a hotel room, toured the endlessly fascinating NOLA that night and the following morning, then allocated an hour or two to resting before the big event.

Ticket taking and the handing out of identifying/entry lanyards took place in the courtyard of the House of Blues situated in the French Quarter.

If there is anything about New Orleans in which to be disappointed (and there isn't much!), it is the absence of significant French elements in the French Quarter, other than street signs with French names, willfully mispronounced by natives of the town. Oh yes, and there are some fine French restaurants with famous chefs, but the overwhelming cuisine in the Quarter is original to New Orleans itself: crawfish, gumbo, jambalaya, muffulettas, and Oysters Rockefeller. French contributions are a merely part of a fusion that combines soul food, Creole, Spanish, Cajun, and Sicilian elements.

Around the courtyard, we saw guests in top hats and goggles, paramilitary uniforms, crinoline petticoats and boots, all in shades of black and brown. We were just starting to get the idea behind steampunk as a style. Thus, we were dressed for a vampire ball (i.e., wearing basically costume-level formal wear). The fact that we fit right in clinched the unspoken link between steampunk and Goth. Both hearkened to an antique age and obsolete belief systems, the world before space flights, instant communication, and modern medicine. Goth would seek to transcend that antiquated world with supernatural affectations pertaining to vampires and witches and ghosts. Steampunk accomplished a similar form of transcendence with anachronistic science fiction: time machines and airships that operated with brass gears and cathode tubes.

Posters were hanging from the gates and fences, featuring the filigreed, top-hatted skull face and copper-colored gears—the logo for the annual event. An outdoor bar was actively serving drinks. Musicians played in one corner of the courtyard and ticketholders milled about gawking at each other's costumes. A small crowd stood by Father Sebastiaan's workstation, observing him attentively craft wearable fangs onto the teeth of a client seated comfortably at his station. When the meet and greet was over, everyone took a break to leave and go prepare for the night's event.

When we returned for the indoor ball, many were dressed in more flamboyant costumes than they had been in the afternoon. Corsetry, gowns, and peasant-girl dress were noted. Some men sported waxed-up handlebar moustaches to go with their vintage aviator outfits. One young woman wore a Medusa crown composed of dozens of little convoluted metallic snakes. Her escort wore a suit of armor.

DJs and live acts went on all night, but the real fun was dancing the night away into morning amidst this ecstatically happy crowd of Goths/steampunks. Eventually exhausted, we crashed for a couple of hours back at the hotel before summoning a taxi at 4:00 a.m. to take us to the airport and, from there, back home.

Steampunk World's Fair 2013

We were in the process of coming to understand the relationship of steampunk with Goth. Perhaps it was costumes. Then along came the Steampunk World's Fair, which we figured could lay it all out for examination: the styles of dress, the eccentric preoccupations, the musical and artistic taste that went with the phenomenon.

Zealous fans of this elaborate branch of geekdom, which includes a contingent of Goths, gathered at two adjacent hotels in central New Jersey for this three-day convention celebrating the peculiar style and mindset of unfulfilled science fiction of the past. The books of Jules Verne (1828–1905) are seminal, providing themes drawn from *Journey to the Center of the Earth*, *Around the World in 80 Days*, and *Twenty Thousand Leagues under the Sea*. Thus, airships, blimps, diving gear, squids and octopi have a revered place in the aesthetic of steampunk.

The retro-futuristic angle of steampunk owes a great deal H. G. Wells (1866–1946) whose book *The Time Machine* introduces the concept of time travel, putting the notion at the disposal of steampunks who imagine an escape, both backward into the nineteenth century and forward into the high-tech future.

The Countess and I strolled the open space between the two hotels called the Goblin Market. This served as a midway where vendors and exhibitors displayed their wares, mostly creative artworks, personal adornments, and home furnishings. These items featured the signature style of steampunk, namely, faux antiques as well as improbably engineered contraptions containing gears and sprockets, ray-guns, submarines, airships, and deep-sea creatures.

Once we signed in and entered, we found the ground level hotel rooms were occupied by more vendors and exhibitors selling such steampunk necessities as walking sticks, corsets, top hats, and brass-accented jewelry.

A fashion show took place, featuring convention goers who displayed their often wildly individualistic, yet always theme-appropriate costumes, attired like characters in an R-rated version of *Willy Wonka* meets *Game of Thrones*.

A marching band wore metallic makeup and performed in a robotic manner. Burlesque shows featured male and plus-size female strippers. A workshop was held on Baritsu, the art of walking stick self-defense. Goth celebrity Aurelio Voltaire hosted an absinthe-tasting event and later reprised his sarcastically worded antifolk song and standup routine at a midnight performance.

FOUNDATIONS OF GOTH-INDUSTRIAL AS I CAME TO UNDERSTAND IT

I had not been paying attention during the early, formative days of the Goth scene. MTV during the 1970s and early '80s had exposed me to punk rock in the most superficial way, but I remained completely unaware of its Gothic-industrial offspring. In my interest to learn the facts of the origins of Goth as a subculture, I looked into the history of Goth rock.

It turns out that the term was first used in 1967 to describe the music of The Doors, which stood distinctly separate from the contemporary, bouncy, optimistic music of the Beatles and the hippies. That struck me as odd because of the decade-long gap between the Doors and what I was coming to understand to be Gothic rock. I suspect that the androgynous and somewhat eerie persona of David Bowie appeared capable of forming a bridge by which punk rock might cross over to Goth.

I considered that the first really Gothic bands and their fans—Bauhaus, Joy Division, the Cure, Siouxsie and the Banshees, et al.—found themselves converging on a certain aesthetic sensibility without conscious self-labeling as Gothic. Rarely is a character or group aware of the movement that they are initiating, let alone the labels that will be applied to them. What counts is how the aggregate population of the subculture that they come to define will see them.

European Influences

Where did the "dark" in the New Dark Age come from? From whence the nostalgia for the bygone era evoked by the term *Gothic* associated as it is with novels from the eighteenth and nineteenth centuries, with crumbling castle ruins and with an ancient tribe of civilization-overturning barbarians?

The Cold War had Europeans (those not already inhabiting the Eastern nations, captive by the Soviet Union) living under the constant threat of invasion by the Red Army—poised on the borders of the West, preparing to complete the imprisonment of the rest of Europe. In America, we lived with the persistent anticipation of a civilization-destroying war with the nuclear-armed Soviets.

The UK experienced these pressures the most intensely. Impoverished by the costs of the Second World War, its cities presented a gray, joyless industrial landscape. The damaged economy brought forth a generation of cynical, disaffected youth who rejected the nationalism and traditions of their collapsing empire for having failed to spare them the squalor left behind by the war. Defying the two-tiered British class system, they embraced their poverty-stricken status by adopting the meager adornments and gear we associate with punk: shaved or partly shaved heads, industrial-style footwear, and patched garments held together with safety pins.

Based on the self-consciously defiant, iconoclastic attitude of punk, it was a short leap to provocative makeup, all-black attire, and the gloomy funereal attitude in honor of the death of societal conventions. The look of Siouxsie Sioux served as a template for that kind of appearance.

As discussed earlier, in the section on Wave Gotik Treffe, in the years preceding the 1989 fall of communism, the punk-rock movement and its new wave / postpunk offshoots of Goth and industrial, were spreading from the US and UK into Western Europe and then finally into the Eastern nations of Soviet captivity. Famous tours by Depeche Mode and the Cure crossed the Iron Curtain where they received fanatical acclaim, severely jeopardizing the Communist Party's hold on the hearts and minds of the people in those countries.

Meanwhile, the other multinational conglomerate of international communism, Yugoslavia was exposed and laid bare by the "over-identification" promulgated by the Slovenian industrial band Laibach, who affected a faux fascistic appearance and staged performances that mocked totalitarianism, militarism, and hypernationalism. Laibach played no small part in fomenting the 1991 secession of Slovenia, the first nation to declare itself independent of the Soviet-style Yugoslav conglomerate. This eventually brought down the whole regime, which had been based upon such kitschy aesthetics and retrograde principles.

Involvement of a musical project in the downfall of tyranny is not unprecedented. During the struggle for independence of Italy in the 1860s, the patriotic opera music of composer Giuseppe Verdi stirred Italians to strive for the overthrow of foreign domination. His name, VERDI, was taken as an acronym as rallying cry for revolutionaries who were promoting Victor Emmanuel for king of Italy, which, in Italian, is written "*V*ittorio *E*mmanuele *R*e *D*'*I*talia" This slogan contributed to the successful rebellion that resulted in the formation of the nation of Italy.

THE ORIGINAL MUSICAL FOUNDATION: BAUHAUS AND JOY DIVISION

In the history of Goth, two musical projects stand out, not only for their spectacularly unique breakthroughs in musical style but for the aura of darkness and eccentricity. More than the Cure, more than Siouxsie and the Banshees, more than the Sisters of Mercy, these two bands—Bauhaus and Joy Division—contributed the essential elements that expanded into Gothic rock and the cultural phenomenon that is Goth.

Peter Murphy and Bauhaus

I attended my umpteenth performance of Peter Murphy at Webster Hall in 2013. Although he had garnered true fame and success as a solo performer, his career began as the lead vocalist for the foundational Goth band Bauhaus, which had disbanded thirty years earlier.

Revivals of the oeuvre of seminal band Bauhaus were highly anticipated and greeted with frenzied enthusiasm whenever they would recur. Resurrections of the full, original band were rare occurrences that would fill large venues or play to sold-out crowds at smaller venues. When Peter Murphy went on tour, much of his set consisted of tracks from the Bauhaus era (1978–1983). Bauhaus's body of work serves as a cornerstone of the Gothic and punk underground musical subculture that overturned the rules of rhythm and melody and, by extension, the style, fashion, and even behavior that had prevailed previously. And no element of it is acclaimed with greater glory than the nine-and-a-half-minute anthem "Bela Lugosi's Dead."

How Bauhaus Came to Define Goth

One night in late 1978, teenage guitarist Daniel Ash, who had been performing in various gigs with different bands and around the Midlands of England, went cruising for a vocalist to join him and his mates. He popped into what was presumably a gay bar. Impressed by the gaunt, epicene male stripper, he approached him and later struck up a deal to create a band, to be joined by Kevin Haskins and, eventually, David J (whose stage name dropped the surname Haskins), Ash's boyhood chums.

The exotic dancer was Peter Murphy, a long-ago friend from Northampton where they both grew up. Murphy had no experience with music or singing, but what they were interested in was his androgynous, angular appearance—an invaluable asset in the glam rock scene of the mid-seventies. They quickly formed a band called the Craze, but soon changed the name for something with more gravity, Bauhaus 1919, for their first gig at a pub on New Year's Eve 1978. The name was chosen as a reference to the ultramodern German art school founded in 1919 and noted for its starkly sterile, eccentric designs. The "1919" was soon dropped, and the band called simply Bauhaus.

I like to imagine a half-serious conversation among the four members of Bauhaus during their earliest recording session in January of 1979, during which one or another of them brought up the name of horror movie star Bela Lugosi, identified with the iconic cinematic persona of undead vampire Dracula from the classic gothic novel of the same name.

"Is Bela Lugosi still alive? Is he dead?" one of them might have asked.

To which the reply would have been, "Bela Lugosi's dead."

And then, using the term used in the iconic movie, he might have added, "Well, actually, *undead*."

The result was their first single, a nine-plus-minute-long, bizarre, mantra-driven dirge that transcended the increasingly popular new-wave style of music, emerging as the first, iconic, and foundational archetype of Goth rock. This was the turning point—the actual birth of Goth as we know it. Earlier postpunk and new-wave artists had been unconventional, but there had been no focus. Siouxsie had worn exaggerated, sinister makeup. Robert Smith of the Cure looked like an androgynous nightmare with his smeared lipstick and rat's nest hair. But Bauhaus's new hit single, with its reference to bats and blood and coffins, had opened a dark path that the main offshoot of postpunk would follow for decades to come. Postpunk would forever be bonded to horror cinema, vampires, gothic literature, and funereal preoccupations.

Bauhaus recorded its first demo consisting of five tracks, one of which was, of course, "Bela Lugosi's Dead." It was released in 1979 and caught the ear of BBC radio disc jockey John Peel, considered the most important presenter of punk, postpunk, electronic, psychedelic, and progressive rock. Peel asked them to record a session for his regular evening show. It aired in early 1980. They were picked up by 4AD Records to record now-famous singles "Dark Entries" and "Terror Couple Kills Colonel," then their first album *In the Flat Field*. In September of 1980, executives of Wax Trax Records booked Bauhaus to perform in Chicago, Illinois.

Three more albums were recorded, one in 1981, one in 1982, and one in 1983. A cover of David Bowie's "Ziggy Stardust," in the 1982 album *The Sky's Gone Out*, skyrocketed that album to near the top of the charts. Bauhaus's performance of "Bela Lugosi's Dead" during the opening credits of the motion picture *The Hunger* arguably captured more attention than costars David Bowie and Catherine Deneuve.

The 1983 motion picture *The Hunger* is either a tedious, uninspired piece of cinema or it is a monumental milestone of today's culture. Actually, it is the latter. The opening scene of this otherwise pedestrian movie introduced the single most influential element of what was to become the Goth, or postpunk culture, when Peter Murphy led the band Bauhaus in the now-iconic song, "Bela Lugosi's Dead (undead, undead, undead)."

That song—atonal, repetitive, and monotonously hypnotic—defined and set the atmosphere for that countercultural movement, namely, Goth, that has persevered and grown into a worldwide phenomenon, spawning countless spin-offs into of the realms of music, art, aesthetics, fashion, and, indeed, lifestyle that permeate the dark world of the major cities and little towns around the world. It was to eventually hurl Bauhaus's vocalist, Peter Murphy, to Olympian status in the Gothic/punk and alternative music pantheon.

Bauhaus went on a tour of Europe and Asia to promote the fourth album *Burning from the Inside* but announced their decision to disband at a show in London a week before its release in 1983.

The year 1998 saw Bauhaus reunite for a *Resurrection* tour. Since then Bauhaus has on several other occasions, reunited, whole or in part, but always with the essential Peter Murphy, for resurrection in the UK and in the States. Another reunion took place in 2005 and several times more. Whenever this occurs, the announcements are greeted with excitement and anticipation; and the venues, large and small, sell out to packed audiences who attend the event with almost religious fervor.

In 2008, the band made a recording comeback with a newly released album of original music *Go Away White*, their first in twenty-five years, sticking to their original delightfully monotonous and discordant style. It was not critically acclaimed, but nonetheless represented a restatement of the singular surviving foundational Goth band's style and would portend increasing, if intermittent, revival of the band as a standard-bearer of the original style that started the whole genre.

Other spin-offs of the band would emerge such as Daniel Ash's and Kevin Haskins' Tones on Tails, and David J's Love and Rockets. Murphy also dabbled in a short-lived but interesting project, *Dali's Car* before committing to his immensely successful and creative solo career.

Peter Murphy and the Undead Life of Bauhaus

Peter Murphy, who served as the lead vocalist of Bauhaus, went on as a soloist after the breakup of the band. No other spin-off from Bauhaus could boast the same level of acceptance and success. He has produced some of the most memorable and beloved songs of the scene, and despite occasional indiscretions, he remains one of the most idolized solo personalities of the scene. His oeuvre contains both richly melodic and raucously rhythmic pieces to accompany his poetic, enigmatic lyrics. In the latter half of 2019, he scheduled a two-week-long residency at Le Poisson Rouge in Manhattan but was taken ill with a heart attack midway through the program.

At the time of *The Hunger*'s cinematic release, Bauhaus had been in existence around five years and was soon to break up. Rather than die, however, Bauhaus entered a state of "undead" (i.e., it had created a legacy, particularly for the charismatic lead singer Peter Murphy, whose solo career seemed to rise like Bela Lugosi from his coffin, slowly, tentatively, then gloriously with his solo debut album, *Should the World Fail to Fall Apart* (1986), followed by eight more studio albums of his original, now-beloved music).

In the thirty-plus years that followed, Murphy has acquired a zealous, almost obsessed, worldwide following that seemingly cannot get enough of his gloomy baritone, poetic lyrics, and unique musical style, which contains a mix of lush, seductive melodies and harsh Bauhaus-flavored elements.

In early August this year, he settled in for a two-weeks-long residency at the Le Poisson Rouge in New York City, covering most of his original work. Some of these tracks had rarely or never been performed live before. Eleven performances were scheduled, including all but one, *Unshattered* (2004), of his solo albums, plus one night devoted to his greatest hits, one to Bauhaus, and one to covers of David Bowie. Such a monumental project, covering the essential body of work of such a significant artist was a milestone in the history of Gothic rock. Besides providing a spectacular musical experience, this major project helps us to understand his unique success and the fanatical following Peter Murphy had accrued in his career, which began in 1986.

I was privileged to interview PM by phone, speaking to him at his home in Istanbul. He was able to retain a decent sense of modesty despite the adulation earned by always attaining the highest levels of excellence by putting forth the maximum effort, sincerity, and generosity toward his audience. He spoke with enthusiasm about the grueling and multifaceted residency project he was about to undertake at Le Poisson Rouge.

Midway through his week-and-a-half NYC residency of nightly performances, Peter Murphy suffered a physical near-collapse. On the fifth event, he performed the *Cascade* album. The performance of this, the fifth studio album, the midpoint of his thirty-plus-year solo career, which had produced nine studio albums, took place at the halfway point in this challenging and strenuous residency. It is the favorite of many of his fans and contains one of the most frequently requested and performed of all his songs, "I'll Fall with Your Knife." After performing each and every track from that spectacular album and despite the arduous nature of the set, he added the raucous and demanding "Low Room" as an encore.

Cascade was released in the tenth year of his solo career. The album reveals that by then he had reached the zenith in his abilities for composing mysterious and romantic poetry, sung in his rich, finely modulated baritone matched with delicious, melodious hooks and riding upon hypnotic, compelling rhythms that would mark his signature style. As an album, it said a lot about why he had risen to such heights in the estimation of his fan base.

One cannot help but note his obvious dedication to his art in particular as well as to music in general. He had chosen to open for him that night a stunningly original, unique performer Soriah, a costumed *tuvan*, or throat-singer, who thrilled the audience with Siberian, Hindu, and Tibetan chants, employing indigenous instruments and electronic wizardry, to say nothing of his amazing vocal prowess. One could say that Peter Murphy's selecting Soriah was an edifying gift he bestowed upon his fans. The same could be said of his carefully produced album *Dust* (2002), scheduled for the following night, which enhanced our appreciation of Near Eastern melodies and rhythms.

Peter Murphy, the ultimate performer, connects with his audience on a casual and friendly basis, joking amicably from the stage with frankness and familiarity. But he always turns serious and professional when he delivers each song with intensity and virtuosity. Regardless of conditions, he never lags or fails in his efforts to belt out the lyrics forcefully when called for or soothingly in tightly controlled, low, intimate tones when appropriate. It is this commitment to performance standards, above all, that accounts for the zeal and warmth that Peter Murphy engenders in his fans.

No, he is not a household name in the mainstream world of Bruce Springsteen and Mick Jagger. But to the sophisticated connoisseur of the alternative music scene, he is all the more precious: this brilliant singer-songwriter who sits atop their highly personal, semihidden world. To those who consider him the godfather of Goth, he is the greatest performer of all.

On Tuesday, August 13, 2019, Peter Murphy suffered a heart attack (a myocardial infarction), effectively ending his NYC residency. He was admitted to Lenox Hill Hospital, where coronary artery stents were placed. Months later, after he had recovered, he rescheduled each of those missed performances.

Joy Division

The second band we must consider at the roots of Gothic rock and Goth is Joy Division. In the spring of 1976, punk-rock fans Bernard Sumner and Peter Hook attended a Sex Pistols show at the Manchester Lesser Free Trade Hall. Inspired by the Pistols' iconoclastic disregard for standards and with no aspirations toward musicianship, they set out to form their own band. Sumner bought a guitar and Hook borrowed a considerable amount to buy a bass. They recruited Terry Mason, who acquired a drum set, and placed an ad for a vocalist in a record store in Manchester. Ian Curtis replied to the ad and was accepted largely on the basis of being easy to get along with.

They made their debut opening for the Buzzcocks in the spring of 1977, calling themselves Warsaw in homage to Bowie's song, "Warszawa," with Tony Tabac on drums. Steve Brotherdale of the punk-rock band Panik would replace him. But Brotherdale was not easy to get along with, so one night they pulled their vehicle to the side of the road, and when he got out to check for a flat tire, they drove off and left him.

Shortly after, a former classmate of Ian Curtis, Stephen Morris, took over on drums. In an expression of iconoclasm, the band changed their name from Warsaw to Joy Division, the name used during World War II to describe German-forced brothel camps. It appears now that in a botched attempt to, in some way, mimic the

Sex Pistols. With very limited instrumental skills, they stumbled into an original and unique sound. This served to perfectly accompany Curtis's dark, poetic lyrics and baritone voice that sounded as if he was always on "the edge." Edge of what? Despair? Enlightenment? The matchup was unique and spoke to the heart of confused and disillusioned youth. Thus Joy Division was born. Joy Division produced two studio albums, both of which won gold awards from the British Phonographic Industry.

They drew the attention of producers and managers and even RCA Records. They began making recordings both independently and under contract labels. Critics praised their creativity. Curtis appeared on the cover of the January 1979 issue of *NME* (London's *New Music Express* magazine). They conducted a tour of Europe with rave reviews. Around that time, Curtis began having epileptic seizures, some during performances while onstage.

In 1980, Joy Division was scheduled to tour the US and Canada. The band was seen as having the potential to be as big as the Beatles of a decade earlier. Curtis's failing marriage imploded, and his pregnant wife filed for divorce. He was under severe emotional conflict from the attentions of a female journalist and follower of the band. By then, his epilepsy had become uncontrolled, and his mental health worsened under the influence of the antiseizure medication phenobarbital, a potent barbiturate.

Ian Curtis—Original portrait painting by Doktor John (2017)

On the eve of departure for the North American tour, Ian Curtis ended his life by hanging himself. His grim, cold, forlorn lyrics had seemed to foretell this gloomy finale. The tragic, premature death of this talented, anguished artist and the demise of Joy Division were so profoundly felt with such frustration that it lifted Curtis and the band to immortality and instant iconic status. Thus, the musical realm of postpunk was born. Soon after, the surviving members of Joy Division reorganized as New Order, a poppy, dance band relying heavily of electronic and synthesized tracks. New Order continues to this day.

There is no way to overstate the reverence in which Joy Division is held by the current generation. In 2016, the cover band Disorder performed "A Tribute to the Sounds of Joy Division" at the dive bar and performance space Dingbatz in Clifton, New Jersey, to an audience of about sixty. Among them were a handful of late-teen, early-twentysomething girls who not only responded with squeals of delight when they recognized the first few notes of a given Joy Division piece, but who accurately lip-synched the lyrics of songs that were released around the time when these girls' parents were in elementary school.

WHAT ABOUT INDUSTRIAL MUSIC?

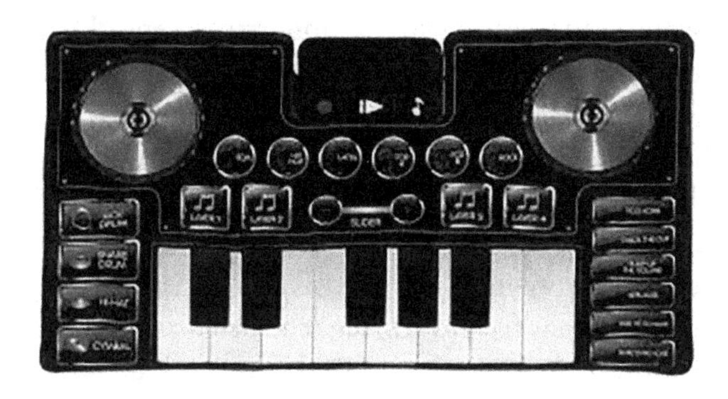

The recording of noise and ambient sounds dates back to the early twentieth century and was called concrete music for including samples that were not produced by instruments but by other sources. The first electronic pop composition, a 1957 recording titled "Song of the Second Moon," was released on the album *The Fascinating World of Electronic Music* in 1963.

The first wave of music to be named industrial came from a London-based company actually named Industrial Records, founded in 1975. The artists under that label produced experimental music with altered instruments, noise, and electronic sounds. They engaged in performance art and took names like Throbbing Gristle, Leather Nun, Non, and Cabaret Voltaire. Above all, they rejected mainstream culture, art, and bourgeois values. They took the countercultural attitude of punk rock and performed it on electronic instruments and noisemakers. The early bands under that label were no longer getting much play in clubs when I entered the scene in the early nineties but were held in a remote esteem as legends.

By splicing in the sounds of machinery, traffic, clips from news broadcasts, cinema, conventional recordings, etc., industrial music sounded a cacophonous echo of automated, mechanized, modern life. As the genre evolved in the 1980s, it held on to the original iconoclastic attitude and unconventional methods but settled into a rhythm-based, dance club-friendly mode, merging, as it were, the elements of punk and disco.

By the 1990s, there was less emphasis on the avant-garde and more on commercial appeal in the industrial scene. Diverse styles broke out. Skinny Puppy, Front 242, and Nitzer Ebb went in for apocalyptic, dehumanized soundscapes over punishing jackhammer beats. Nine Inch Nails effected a crossover into popular radio and MTV with funky synthesized sounds and the in-your-face presence of Trent Reznor's quirky vocal narratives. Ministry, initially a synth-pop band, interwove heavy-metal guitar riffs and patently offensive lyrics to produce a style that fit into the big tent that was industrial metal.

That industrial music should find wide appeal, albeit within a limited demographic, is somewhat counterintuitive. Musically, most industrial music is so pared down, so devoid of the customary features of music in the conventional sense as to be closer to what most people define as noise. That goes for stripped-down yelling with little or no melody, as in the works of Nitzer Ebb, or complicated, sonically "dirty" sound of Skinny Puppy or Ministry, with layers of competing electronica, static, distorted voices, reverb, looping, and mechanical noise. Adding to the auditory assault is the frequent resort to harsh, hostile, and abrasive lyrics. The lyrics of Nine Inch Nails are clearly enunciated, angry, despondent, and often riddled with nonsequitors. Those of Skinny Puppy are jumbled, random, predominantly negative and enigmatic. Throbbing Gristle's are abrasive and psychotic.

Friends and relatives expressed bewilderment and concern at my acquiring appreciation of and attachment to industrial music.

They expressed fear that such music, saturated with nonmelodious noise and vitriolic lyrics, would have a negative effect on my mood and thinking. In fact, the opposite occurred. Instead, I found that the chaos and belligerence of industrial music expressed negative feelings that I didn't need to express nor even harbor within my own heart. It was like the sound and fury of industrial artists and bands liberated me from the need to indulge in negative thoughts and emotions. They had taken the burden upon themselves of howling out grievances against the tumult; the angst of the modern, mechanized world; as well as the social dislocations in my personal life. They bore that cross on my behalf, expressing the existential anguish and gloom of postmodern industrialized society, so that I had no need to do so.

Skinny Puppy is, in my opinion, the par excellence example of industrial music, one of the founders of the industrial genre. The group started in 1982 in Canada's West Coast city of Vancouver, British Columbia, its central, creative core consisting of cEvin Key and vocalist Nivek Ogre, with intermittent participation by a number of famous-in-their-own right luminaries from the world of techno-industrial and Goth music. The rotating cast of singers, instrumentalists, and technicians has kept Skinny Puppy's output endlessly innovative, but always with the signature style with which the project is identified. A recurring theme is animal rights and anti-vivisection.

In addition, Skinny Puppy has developed an over-the-top, live-stage approach that aims to shock, confuse, and mystify audiences with costumes, unconventional lighting, and stylized acts. Images of war, ecological disaster, and man's inhumanity to man are featured in projected sequences while Nivek Ogre sings and performs antics on stage in remarkable, elaborate productions.

I—mostly alone in the early nineties and then in later years accompanied by the Countess—had numerous occasions to see Skinny Puppy perform live onstage. A fairly typical show we attended took place in 2009 at the Nokia Center off Times Square. Nivek Ogre came onstage horrifyingly stooped over an invalid walker, masked, and wearing either a huge dunce cap (or Ku Klux Klan hood, depending on how one viewed it). The entire stage was illuminated by undecipherable flashes of motion-picture images flickering in stroboscopic fashion. The band performed their classic masterpieces with very clear vocalization of the enigmatic lyrics arising out of layers of rich electronics. Ogre's costume came off in a series of unveilings throughout the hour-long performance, each time revealing yet another creepy mask or garment underneath. After about an hour, they took a break and returned with their most sought anthem, "Worlock," followed by an unfamiliar experimental number and reaching a climax with "Far Too Frail" a track dating back to 1984, which could be an archetype for their vast body of work.

Skinny Puppy's message of existential angst, free-floating hate, political protest, and general madness has been sounding for decades, serving, in varying degrees, as an influential template for the iconoclastic attitude and nihilistic outlook of the Goth subculture. More perhaps than any other band, Skinny Puppy has acquired an exalted status in the alternative music scene with almost religious devotion and stands atop the pantheon of industrial musicians, which includes the following noteworthies: Ministry, which started out as a poppy, Goth-disco band and became a ferocious, uncensored voice of anarchy and leftism; the sci-fi based Front Line Assembly, a project of former SP member Bill Leeb; and successful mainstream crossover Nine Inch Nails, product of creative genius Trent Reznor.

Nivek Ogre of Skinny Puppy on various stages

THE NYC GOTHIC PUNK AND INDUSTRIAL SCENE

I set about tracing the roots of the NYC Goth scene, which brought me back to a tangled thread originating in the late 1970s and early '80s when disco declined in popularity while punk, synthpop, and minimalism were on the rise. Disco was replaced by electronic dance, house, and techno, representing a minimalist trend that merged with punk, glam, and new wave. Collectively, these eventually came to be seen as constituting alternative music. All styles, which emphasized vocals while continuing to rely upon electronic enhancements, came to be known as postpunk. When postpunk went in the direction of alienation, iconoclasm, and defiance, Gothic rock and the Goth scene were born.

The Greater NYC Goth scene entered a golden age in the early 1990s when numerous clubs began to cater to the growing clientele of dark-music enthusiasts who shared the punk and postpunk sensibility.

Preeminent among these were the Limelight, CBGBs and CB's 313 Gallery, the Pyramid, the Bank, Albion/Batcave at Downtime, Coney Island High, Mother, and others too numerous or too transient to mention. Noteworthy New Jersey clubs included the legendary Pipeline, which reigned in Newark alongside QXT's, and two other North Jersey venues, Aldo's and the Loop Lounge.

Multiband and DJ events occurred here and there in Manhattan at places like Mother, the Batcave, Coney Island High on St. Mark's Place in the East Village, The Pyramid, the Limelight, the Bank at the corner of East Houston Street and Essex and at lesser-known locations. Concept nights appeared under a variety of different names such as Communion, Equilibrium, Downtime, and Mass. Eventually, the preeminent of all these became known as Alchemy, which continued a decade-long run as a weekly event at CB's Gallery under promoters Althea and DJ Jason. In 2006, CBGBs and the next-door CB's Gallery closed as a result of rent/lease disputes with its landlord. Among all these nightclubs, only the Pyramid club survived up until spring of 2021, when it announced it was closing.

The Limelight was a converted Gothic church where all subtypes of society and music took the stage on a nightly, rotating basis, weeknights and weekends for much of the 1990s and 2000s. CBGBs, on the notorious Bowery, was originally founded to host country, bluegrass, and blues. It was taken over by new wave and punk bands, eventually soaring to fame when the Ramones, Patti Smith, Blondie, and the Talking Heads performed there. The storefront next door was designated CB's 313 Gallery, which hosted the long-enduring club night Alchemy, making it ground zero in the Goth, industrial, and darkwave scene. The annual Miss Gothic NYC pageant also took place there, further broadening the cultural spectrum of the underground culture.

Alchemy Monday and CBGBs

In 1996, Althea Ann and DJ Jason cofounded Alchemy, the longest-lasting and historically significant weekly Goth dance club night at CBGBs 313 Gallery. It, in a certain sense, defined the Goth scene in NYC going forward. It lasted well into the new millennium, concluding with its final occurrence in 2006, making Althea Ann, perhaps the most famous and recognized promoter, hostess, and organizer in the NYC Goth club scene. During the pandemic lockdown, I interviewed her by phone and electronically.

Q: When did you first become aware of the dark music scene?

A: My first Goth sighting was when I was around ten years old. While out for a walk with my parents, I caught sight of a black-clad young woman with blue hair. I thought, *Wow! That's beautiful!* The first time I heard Goth music was when I was around thirteen years old. Riding in my parents' car, the radio was tuned to WFNX Boston. Siouxsie's "Cities in Dust" came on. I immediately resolved to purchase the album, one of my first to own. From then, my interest in exploring similar style music began to blossom.

Q: How did you come to make New York your scene?

A: Around 1990, I came to New York for college.

Q: How did you become involved in the nightlife music scene?

A: As a teenager growing up in New England, I had already known my share of punk rock, and I had followed through into the postpunk, Goth rock scene. Through a friend, I landed a job at the Limelight. Nothing had prepared me for the immersive club scene of NYC. There might be a dozen dance clubs attended by thousands literally every night, weekdays as well as weekends. I was dazzled by the spectacle of bizarrely costumed dancers and the ever-changing names, design, and décor of various nights at the Limelight. I had to learn to find my own comfort zone within this new environment.

Q: How deep was your own personal involvement in the goings-on?

A: I distanced myself early from the "club-kid/rave scene" where there was widespread use of recreational drugs. I was obliged to work one night called Rock & Roll Church which featured heavy-metal bands. Those patrons were less than generous with the tips I needed to live on. So instead I fell right in with the Limelight's Goth night, an event called Communion, being promoted by my roommate. I soon looked into other Goth nights going on in the city.

Q: So you didn't limit yourself to the Limelight?

A: The job there had hours that ended at 5:00 a.m. I was only able to attend those other clubs on nights when I didn't work the Limelight. But I made it my business to do so every single one of those nights. I arranged my college schedule to start classes no earlier than 10:00 a.m.

Q: How long did that go on?

A: After a year, I had enough of the Limelight and took to the help-wanted pages of the *Village Voice*. Wading through the club listings and musician-wanted ads, I found a job tending bar at CBGBs. It would prove to be not only my home for many years, but the central location in my social life, where I would make friends and develop relationships with talented and truly amazing friends.

Q: How did things go at CBGBs?

A: The focus was on live band performances. My work night tending bar ended around 2:00 a.m., allowing me to visit all the other clubs in town on terms of complimentary, free admission. I attended the Limelight selectively, attending my favorite weekly event, Communion. On other nights I was at the Bank for Realm/Exedor Fridays, various nights at the Pyramid and at Father Jeff's events.

Q: How did tending bar at CBGBs lead to your becoming the promoter, hostess, and organizer that you became?

A: One memorable, but mostly forgotten venue, was a small bar on Houston called Idelwild where James Galus, who went by Saint James, hosted a series of events. One was an after-party where Daniel Ash of Bauhaus made an appearance. It was also where Voltaire (now Aurelio Voltaire) put on his first public performance.

Q: What happened to Idelwild?

A: When James got notice his event was ending, he suggested I start my own night. After pitching the idea to a number of local bars, I struck up a deal with the owner of a bar called The Far Side. My idea was to cover costs by tending bar so that I didn't have to charge admission. I recruited DJ Daniel, well-known for his spinning at the bank. I designed some flyers, Xeroxed them at Kinko's, and launched my night. I called it Tocsin, after the ringing sound an alarm bell makes. It's also the name of a 1984 album by the all-female Goth band X-Mal Deutschland.

Q: How did Tocsin lead to Alchemy?

A: I already had a wide circle of contacts from working at the Limelight and CBGBs. DJ Dan was also well-known. The space was small and the atmosphere quirky, like I liked. But eventually, The Far Side got sold to new owners. Tocsin relocated several times to places like Alcatraz on Avenue A and then to the Chameleon Lounge, a karaoke bar. When the last of these went out of business, I took advantage of my relationship with CBGBs to set up a regular night in the adjacent CBGB's Gallery. I called it Alchemy, alluding to the idea of a fusion of elements and also echoing the first two letters of my name.

Q: How was Alchemy set up?

A: The Gallery space had a small stage as well as a sound system that allowed me to book live acts. My previous employment at CBGBs was an advantage in establishing a relationship with the management. The highly supportive owner, Hilly Kristal, never fully grasped the idea of a Goth theme. From time to time, he would ask me, "How's that death metal night of yours going?"

Alchemy maintained an intimate, insider feel, where mainly those in the know gathered with a sprinkling of out-of-town curiosity seekers were also welcomed. We tried to give new and obscure artists opportunity to perform. The DJ playlist ran from typical Goth-industrial standards and sometimes included silly oddities and eighties throwback tunes.

Q: All fun and games, was it?

A: My memories also include the demanding nature of running a club night. Calling and emailing bands, juggling schedules, designing promotional flyers, having them printed and seeing to their distribution. And that's not to say anything about the physical tasks of hauling equipment to the place for each occurrence of Alchemy and then folding everything up and hauling it all back out at closing in the early morning hours. There was never a lot of money, but there was the joy and satisfaction of engaging with friends who shared our taste in music and that particular brand of socializing. Those benefits have lasted me right up to the present.

Q: Have you any one special memory? Any turning point?

A: One night in 1997, someone dropped off flyers for an event in Germany, one that was previously obscure to me and little known, if at all, in the NYC Goth scene. It was the now famous Wave Gotik Treffen (WGT), the largest meeting of Goths from around the world. Convincing an old high school friend to accompany me, we made the trip to Leipzig, Germany, where I discovered a vast

> new world of dark, alternative music. I was soon importing foreign recordings to air and recruiting bands from overseas to perform on Alchemy's live stage. Repeated visits, year after year served to transform downtown NYC's underground music scene. I know it prompted others to visit the WGT annually.

DJ Jason and the Miss Gothis NYC Pageants

Jason had made a name for himself as a curator of Gothic-industrial music on college radio going back as far as 1986, and was a contributor to Goth-themed magazines and radio shows right through 2005.

In addition to Alchemy, of which he was cofounder, DJ Jason deejayed, produced or coproduced, and promoted club events at Coney Island High (Wasteland and Sabotage), Acme Underground (Shadowplay), Mother (Long Black Veil), the Bank (Flesh and Blood), Korova Lounge (Nightshift), and the Pyramid (Ward 6).

Among the most spectacular events was the Miss Gothic NYC Pageant, held annually in the late 1990s into 2000. These were hosted by Alchemy and emceed by jokester Voltaire, who used his ironic wit to keep both the participants and the contestants from taking themselves too seriously. Judges included former Miss Gothics, local rock stars, and DJs. Seven or eight of the scene's most beautiful and exemplary Goths competed on evening wear, talent, and ability to fend off Voltaire's not-so-standard beauty-pageant questions.

The most and the least entertaining parts of each pageant occurred during the displays of talent or lack thereof. Attired in mainly black outfits ranging from tattered rags to cinematic vampire to cyberpunk dominatrix, some read morose poetry, others displayed their artwork. At one pageant, a gentleman contestant held up for display his man-sized wardrobe of feminine attire. One contestant killed what seemed an eternity mixing, occasionally spilling, and eventually serving what they purported was the perfect martini.

Better moments during the talent portion came when recently out lesbian Allison acted out a "spoken word" denunciation of a former boyfriend; when an exotic beauty Emily in a catsuit and strap-on lip-synced and danced like a wild banshee on stage; and when that evening's winner, Alexia, displayed her prowess with a yo-yo while wearing a corset, garter belt, stockings, and little else.

At other pageants, multiple contestants presented their skills at belly-dancing. One of the candidates turned the tables on Voltaire, donning a beard herself and doing a great job of satirizing his satirical persona. A particular pageant winner earned her title while capturing the spirit of the event by her displayed talent of consuming a whole bottle of Jaegermeister while stripping down to her most display-worthy assets. All we spectators in the audience were relieved to see the contents of that bottle reemerge the way it went in, saving our winner from the potentially toxic effects it might have had.

Jason hosted and deejayed at his event called Absolution, which took place most notably in the basement of CBGBs and at the Limelight, where he also deejayed Communion and collaborated with Father Sebastiaan for several Sabretooth-sponsored events. DJ Jason also spun at the Court of Lazarus at various locations, and he hosted Gothic New Year's Eve for several years at CBGBs Gallery and Basement.

After Alchemy ended in 2006, DJ Jason continued to deejay, promote, and produce at Fontana's, the Boulevard Tavern, Identity, Happy Ending, and Uncle Mike's.

The 2004 Goth Awards Ceremony

In December of 2004, while Alchemy was still going strong, DJ Jason and Althea hosted an awards ceremony at CBGB's Gallery. Fifty or sixty pierced, tattooed, and flamboyantly costumed Goths were in attendance to watch as judges selected the top DJs, club promoters, musicians, bartenders, and bouncers of the scene.

Aurelio Voltaire served as the emcee. He started off the event with a rendition of his satirical piece, the hilarious "Vampire Club," which debunks the subset of Goths that role play at being vampires, following which he went into a sarcastic stand-up skit in the same vein.

Hal Gould and his staff at Albion/Batcave received a number of awards; and Thera, of the band Folk Fiction, was selected as top lead female vocalist. It was my distinct honor to present the award for number one male lead vocalist to Myke Hideous. The awards were only half tongue in cheek. They represented a way of showing recognition for many who struggled with underfunding and tight schedules to support the scene so dear to the hearts of many lovers of music and nightlife.

The event drove home my realization that a major discrepancy existed between the sinister appearance versus the civilized behavior of these basically genteel people, the Goths of NYC. Despite the dental fangs, chrome spikes, and ghoulish makeup, these were sociable, talented, and artistic kids. They perhaps had not have been popular in school or the neighborhoods where they grew up, but they surely found acceptance in a community that valued creativity, nonconformity, and every deviant form of personal lifestyle. And they all understood that providing support by attending events like this was critical to the survival of the scene that sustained them as individuals.

CULTURAL CORNERSTONES OF THE NYC GOTH SCENE

Museums

Morbid Anatomy Museum

Founded in 2014, the Morbid Anatomy Museum in Brooklyn had a brief, but lasting, influence on the NYC Goth scene by materializing and housing, for a few short years, the collections, exhibitions, and community events that went beyond the nightclubs, concert halls, and annual conventions that make up the basic experience of the scene. It represented the brick-and-mortar embodiment of director Joanna Ebenstein's *Morbid Anatomy* blog (started in 2007) and its offshoot the Morbid Anatomy Library (started in 2008) and originally housed at the gallery Proteus Gowanus. Ms. Ebenstein is an endearingly sweet human with a powerful intellect and aesthetic sense and the author of many books on morbid themes, anatomy included.

Building on the interests forthcoming from these sources, the museum housed collections and hosted exhibitions of highly unusual nature. It focused on the artifacts, practices, interests, and phenomena that normally fall between the cracks of ordinary academic research. It covered rituals surrounding death, carnival-show magic, cabinets of curiosity, anatomical specimens and models, outsider art, and bizarre collections. Thus, taxidermy, both conventional and outlandish, played a recurring role in both the standing collection and passing exhibitions. Often the emphasis was on anatomical abnormalities, as the name of the museum would suggest. Lifelike, medical-school quality instructional models and antiquated surgical implements were frequently on display. But the exhibits were diverse in the extreme. Oddball collections by eccentric individuals including somebody's gathered and arranged hoard of brushes, brooms, and the like. A talking mummy in a coffin took up residence in the main gallery for a while. One could walk around and inspect the trick box in which a magician's assistant might safely hide while multiple swords were driven through it.

The Countess and I attended numerous lectures and presentations starting back in the days when events began at Proteus Gowanus and continued as the museum grew in popularity and acquired the space on Brooklyn's Third Avenue. We frequently recruited guests to come with us to events. We became even more intensely involved when the museum took up residence at an accessible location in Brooklyn. No sooner did I learn about the need that the museum had for what they called docents that I was right on it. I volunteered promptly and was appointed a docent (a fancy name for a guide and teacher), but it wasn't as glorified as that. A docent could sit at a table doing work as long as he/she was keeping an eye on the exhibit. Or if a docent felt like doing so, he/she could hand out printed tour-guide literature and follow the patrons around pointing things out and explaining the displays. I was determined to be the latter.

One of the many exhibitions hosted by the museum, and one that really captured the essence of the museum's mission, was *The Collector's Cabinet.* The contributors were antique dealers, eccentrics, and hoarders plus a few medical professionals. The range of items on display was eclectic, to say the least, including painted wooden religious figures, dental models, séance props, a disarticulated skeleton, taxidermy specimens, and anatomical charts.

Each collector spoke briefly about the history and significance of the various pieces in their unique collection that they had lent to the museum for this exhibit. The famous Evan Michelson, costar of the TV series *Oddities* and co-owner of the then-prominent NYC antiques boutique, demonstrated a pair of artificial arms that allowed a railroad brakeman to return to work after a terrible accident in which he lost his own natural arms.

Another exhibit, called *House of Wax*, presented a spectacular opportunity for museum goers to experience the quintessence of the Morbid Anatomy's mission. The Countess and I attended the opening night. Custom craftsman and bone collector Ryan Matthew Cohn served as curator of the exhibition that featured a collection of wax figures, which he was fortunate enough to obtain from a long-defunct German *panopticum*, actually a nineteenth-century museum of sorts. He spoke at length about the provenance and historical significance of his acquisition. He led us in a champagne toast to kick things off. He explained that in the nineteenth century and early twentieth century, before the advent of cinema and related media, entertainment seekers and those in pursuit of knowledge outside their limited scope used to pay to attend waxwork venues where they could view highly realistic effigies representing everything about which they harbored morbid curiosity disguised as academic interest.

Joanna Edenstein (second from left) and crew at Morbid Anatomy

He had obtained access to the assemblage from Castan's panopticum, which was in business in Berlin from 1869–1922 and contains life-sized anatomical abnormalities (with an emphasis on genitalia and private parts) plus exaggerated caricature busts of human ethnic examples and the death masks of famous historical figures (Napoleon, Kaiser Wilhelm I, Mary Queen of Scots).

At the center of the exhibition were two examples of Anatomical Venus, accurate yet idealized, complete and full-sized human female figures with their innards revealed, all in wax.

Although a variety individuals attended these and other Morbid Anatomy Museum exhibitions, a significant plurality were black-clad Goths. These two exhibits captured the very core mission of the museum, and in so doing, they both catered to the interests and added to the enlightenment of the NYC Goth community.

I was pleased at how easily I fit in with the permanently avant-garde Brooklyn crowd, owing mainly to how open-minded and friendly they are as a rule. The visitors, on the other hand, were decidedly more variable in these attitudes. For the year or two during which I served as a docent, I came to recognize certain recurring types. Perhaps surprisingly, my favorites were enthusiastic elderly ladies. Some of them were familiar with outré matters, but whether or not they were, even if they were completely naïve, they opened their eyes at what was on display and were eager to learn about it. Not so elderly men. I took it to have been an exaggerated attempt to convey that they would rather be talking sports or money with the guys, not bored to death in a quirky museum. I came to recognize the consistent elderly male attitude (i.e., reluctance to show interest in what's quirky), to wit, brush it off and move on.

One enthusiastic mature lady from Brooklyn dressed like she was visiting the theater had been enjoying the exhibit but wondered, almost suspiciously, why there was so much religious iconography. I got the impression she was concerned that the statues of saints and the presence of religious trinkets might indicate disrespect for the religion itself. I assured her that it was due to the importance of religion in issues surrounding death, which was after all, a major theme of the museum. That seemed to make her more comfortable. What she suspected was actually true in a sense. The museum had a definite tongue-in-cheek skepticism in putting items on display, an attitude of looking back at human foibles with amusement as well as curiosity. The museum had to maintain an attitude of ingenuous indifference toward conventional values.

In my opinion, the Morbid Anatomy Museum was the highest, single, dedicated expression of Goth intellectual and aesthetic aspiration that the scene ever produced. I can't say that Joanna was Goth, but she was along the same path as Goths: yearning for meaning. And when the time finally came for me to wed, after a decade-long engagement, the Countess, my soul mate and companion in my travels through the New Dark Age, we held our reception at the venue that was closest to our hearts: the Morbid Anatomy Museum.

Art exhibits with themes of death, the afterlife, and such actually continued after the 2016 demise of the Morbid Anatomy Museum, when the institution closed permanently. It then took the form of live lectures and demonstrations at various host venues. Eventually, the Morbid Anatomy Library relocated to Industry City in Brooklyn, and museum's educational program went mainly virtual.

Wedding Cake

A Special Event at Morbid Anatomy: The Andy Harriman Lecture on the Brief History of Goth

One supporter and shining light associated with the Morbid Anatomy Museum is Andi Harriman, unquestionably a celebrity Goth. She is a world-hopping musicologist DJ and the author of numerous articles on the Gothic music and cultural scene, both in print and in electronic media. Her magnum opus, *Some Wear Leather Some Wear Lace: The World Compendium of Postpunk and Goth in the 1980s*, is the definitive reference book on the origin, meaning, and evolution of the Goth subculture.

In April 2016 Ms. Harriman gave a lecture at the museum. Following is a summary of her lecture entitled "Goth 101." She spoke just under an hour, accompanying her extensive historical account with abundant photographic documentation.

The history of Goth proves to be voluminous, but Andi Harriman puts forward the thesis that the punk cultural movement of the 1970s, with its iconoclastic philosophy and raw musical style set the stage for the inevitable rise of the more wide-ranging and varied, but interrelated styles of the early eighties called postpunk. Out of this conglomerate of musical (and fashion) styles came Goth, a sort of apotheosis of an ancient and fundamental cultural thread, Gothic, that had run through Western civilization for millennia.

She traced roots of the name *Goth* back to marauding nomad pagan tribes, the Goths and Ostrogoths, then the architecture that these former barbarians referred to as Gothic and identified with the period of Europe's Dark Ages. Later, it became associated with ruins and decay, and sometimes served as the backdrop for morbid-themed literature centered on haunted castles, seductive vampires, and themes of emotional despair.

Early cinema continued feeding the undercurrent of dark glamour, featuring such "vamps" as Theda Bara, whom some call the first Goth girl. Ghastly musical-performance art like that of Screamin' Jay Hawkins, Alice Cooper, and the Bowie fertilized the postpunk substrate, eventually giving rise to the dark style of music that we now recognize as Goth rock. Much more information was imparted, drawing largely from Ms. Harriman's book.

More Museums and Galleries

The Fuse Gallery

Long since gone is the Fuse Gallery, uniquely situated in the back walk-through behind the (also gone) Lit Lounge on Second Avenue in the East Village. Cutting-edge art with a punkish or Gothic flavor prevailed. Many artists who exhibited at the Fuse had some connection to the alternative music scene such as Winston Smith, designer of the cover art for Dead Kennedys' album *In God We Trust*, and Mark Mothersbaugh, singer for the eccentric rock band Devo.

In March of 2002, Fuse held an exhibition of the works by Swiss artist H. R. Giger, famous for creation of the monsters from the films *Alien* and *Species*, hosted by the artist himself. The crowd of attendees included NYC alternative art types, some in fine attire but most in either punkish garb or straight-out Goth costumery. On the walls were mounted his early pen-and-ink works featuring gargoylish figures with his characteristic anatomical distortions that include Dali-esque elongation and transformations of one body part into another: fingers become legs, heads become buttocks, torsos open to reveal twisted insides. Hanging from the ceiling was a huge bat-winged angel with an elongated, melon-like head, a female torso, and mermaid-like tail, ending with a gaping cloaca.

The room was dominated by a centrally placed two-meter tall, silvery metallic female figure that serves as the microphone stand for the nu-metal band Korn.

Other female forms around the room echoed Egyptian style. Framed monochrome works of ink on aluminized surfaces showed images both erotic and nightmarish. Giger's work provides a surreal hell inhabited by cybernetic humanoid forms condemned to claustrophobic mechanical confinements by an excess of carnal lust. Just what Goths appear to love viewing or a gruesome look at where technology was taking us in this increasingly artificial and electronic New Dark Age. The exhibit and the demographic of the attendees served to confirm H. R. Giger as a Goth icon.

Last Rites Gallery

Last Rites Gallery was operated by tattoo artist Paul Booth until the Covid lockdown. It was located on Manhattan's West Thirty-Eighth Street and specialized in dark surrealism in its many media and forms. The periodic opening nights were generally peopled with artists and art students, Goths, punks, and ink-adorned inhabitants of the metropolitan demimonde that browsed or shopped the exquisitely, sometimes uncomfortably, explicit works rendered in paint, ink, and sculpture, always with a surrealist bent. The gallery and the world-famous tattoo parlor that helped support it were closed by the Covid-19 pandemic and related restrictions.

Museum at the Fashion Institute of Technology

The Countess and I attended the Museum at the Fashion Institute of Technology's first exhibition devoted to Gothic style in fashion titled *Gothic: Dark Glamour* in 2009. The stereotypical idea of black-clad teenagers served as a starting concept. Victorian mourning attire was presented as having initiated the fashion style and then elaborated via vampire cinematic portrayals. Evoking the decadent elegance of gothic novels, it introduced the mode of wearing anachronistic evening attire, with men in self-consciously retro formal wear and women in elaborate, voluminous, layered evening gowns, almost always in black or shockingly intense colors.

Veils, masks, and corsetry were said to reinforce the idea of isolation as a subtle expression of existentialist uniqueness. Goth fashion was described as being a way of expressing feelings of alienation and otherness that are at the heart of the subculture.

We learned that Goth fashion engages with the recent past by drawing on punk and glam rock but is also seen reaching well back to the Victorian era and before to incorporate, at the extreme end, medieval, and even barbarian, battle dress. At the same time, there is a leap forward into a futuristic, sci-fi look, with the intention of adding to the sought-after appearance of the subculture.

Goths were shown to draw on a cabinet of curiosities for accessories, adorning themselves with elements of religious iconography (crosses, images of saints, prayer beads); nature (bats, feathers, wings, and bird skulls); human skulls, skeletal parts, and death's head symbols; and anything expressing themes of death, time, and transcendence.

The Museum of Sex

Located on Manhattan's Fifth Avenue, the MoSex has featured numerous ongoing shows as well as the standing collection of interest to the Goth-industrial subculture including a year-long exhibition *Punk Lust: Raw Provocation*. Besides featuring a collection of artworks, film, garments, etc., the exhibition drew attention to punk rock's elements of collapsing gender norms, stereotypes, and its confrontation with puritanical morality. Other exhibits of specific interest included surrealist artists' works like those of Leonora Fini that challenged gender roles and expectations. The Museum of Sex was one of the few institutions that appear to have survived the pandemic lockdown of 2020–2021.

MoMA
Tim Burton Exhibition at MoMA

An admired artist of the Goth scene is Tim Burton. Myke Hideous and I attended an exhibition of his art at MoMA around the same time as the Nitzer Ebb concert. Some people only know of him as a maker of gothic fantasy and horror films, and indeed, elements of his cinema art were included, but the exhibit went much farther in laying out the creative produce of Tim Burton's mind and why it is held in high esteem within the Goth scene.

The exhibition tried to convey the enormous and diverse body of his work. Besides being known for his motion pictures like *Beetlejuice* and *Batman*, he was prolific and gifted with pen and ink on paper and on canvas from very early in his life. Just as his movies seek to bridge the gap between childlike innocence and real horror, so too his witty and lighthearted drawings are filled with fantasy creatures with dislocated eyeballs, predatory clowns, and critters with pointy teeth. The parallels with the perpetually adolescent Goth psyche are unmistakable.

There were portraits he penned of select celebrities like Alice Cooper, Vincent Price, and Joey Ramone making clear Burton's affinity for pop culture. But most of the drawings were of aggressive toys, nightmarish yet comical fantasy creatures, and nameless humans with distorted body parts. All are done in wiggly shapes drawn with squiggly lines as if by Aubrey Beardsley intoxicated with absinthe or by Edward Gorey if drawn with his left hand. Life-size models from his motion pictures like the Catwoman's catsuit, the giant menacing jack-o'-lantern from *Nightmare before Christmas*, and an antlered ape head from *Planet of the Apes* seemed to suggest a common thread—Burton's signature preoccupations. I was sure that I could recognize it, but I struggled to articulate it.

The exhibit told me much about the New Dark Age in which we were living, one in which the nightmarish fears of childhood can come to real life in some form during adulthood.

MILESTONE PERFORMANCES

I attended countless performances in my role as reporter of all things Goth-industrial for the *Aquarian*. Some stand out for their significance, either for the subculture or for me as an individual.

Throbbing Gristle

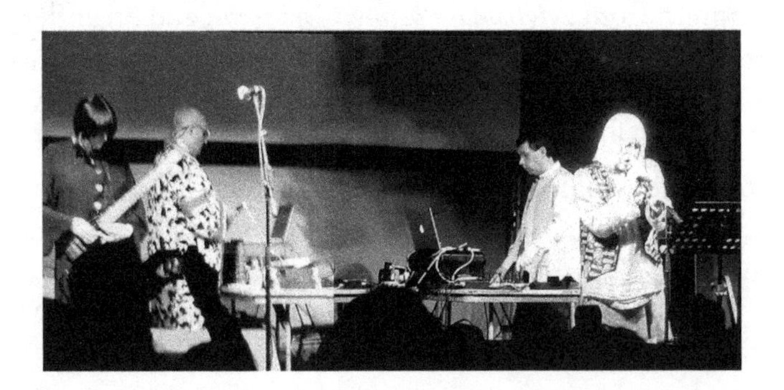

In early 2009, I learned that Throbbing Gristle, one of the most unusual and enigmatic bands (in a genre that is loaded with unusual and enigmatic bands) would be performing at the Brooklyn Masonic Temple. Always mentioned as one of the founders of Industrial Records, along with Cabaret Voltaire and Monte Cazazza, Throbbing Gristle, is an archetypical industrial band making subversive art and music.

Recruiting my younger son Dan to accompany me, we headed over to Brooklyn, eager to witness this icon of the alternative music realm. Originating as a performance art group and self-publishing under the label Industrial Records, Throbbing Gristle was notorious for extremes of harsh, dark, and enigmatic themes; gender-bending and Dada-esque musical; lyrical and visually confusing presentations. Although by then senior citizens and with sex-change transitions behind them, they were still able to recreate the sound and fury if not the original spark of radical cultural subversion that made them founders of the movement.

The audience stood dutifully for an hour-long opening film. *In the Shadow of the Sun*, a nonnarrative of grainy, overexposed footage showing shadowy, silhouetted figures moving in slow motion against poorly defined scenes of destruction. Double exposure allowed bright-red images of roaring flames to be layered over serene landscapes suggesting hell on earth. Close-ups of a man applying feminine makeup and a finger pecking at a typewriter made repeated appearances between shots of grit and grime. Dazzling bright backgrounds with dark figures in the foreground might have been meant to denote the title of the film. An hour was about enough to get the idea. And then some!

At 11:00 p.m., the typical starting time for shows of this nature, the musicians were welcomed on stage with loving enthusiasm by industrial enthusiasts and bewildered admiration by youngsters who were not born yet when Throbbing Gristle tried to overthrow the order of civilization and the music industry in the late seventies. Vocalist Genesis P-Orridge, a matronly yet glamorous transgendered woman flaunted a platinum blond pageboy hairdo and surgically-enhanced feminine features, displaying rage and ferocity usually associated with heavy-metal front men.

The opening number, "Very Friendly," consisted of a fifteen-minute narrative that turned gory, delivered in a bizarre manner over a repetitive rhythmic track of electronic static produced by bathrobe-clad "Sleazy" Christopherson and Chris Carter while Cosey Fanni Tutti abused her guitar.

Other entries in the hour-long set featured mesmerizingly mechanical and, at times, tribal beats. The set ended with the chaotic and deranged "Discipline," with no less hypnotic a pounding, crashing rhythm, over which P-Orridge repeatedly screamed the word *discipline*.

By this stage in my journey into the iconoclastic world of the Goth-industrial counterculture, I was neither surprised nor repelled, not comprehending of the message to be gleaned other than sheer subversion of the world-as-it-is. But I understood that, foundational as Throbbing Gristle was, it was also out on the furthest extreme of that subculture that it was partially responsible for spawning.

A Concert by Nitzer Ebb

An acquaintance passed me word that English industrial band Nitzer Ebb was performing one night in 2009 at Manhattan's Gramercy Theater as part of the band's tour to promote their latest album, *Industrial Complex*. When front man Douglas McCarthy appeared on stage, he wore a suit, a white shirt, and a tie. In the early 1980s, he would be more likely be dressed in jodhpurs and knee-high boots, affecting a militaristic Germanic look. But the business suit look didn't signal any deviation from their signature musical style: complete absence of melody; harsh, repetitive, mantra-like lyrics shouted over pitiless electronic percussion. The very name Nitzer Ebb is a mystery, evoking a kind of dismal, hard feeling but with no particular meaning.

Some of the set was previously unknown to me, but I was thrilled to hear my favorites from their repertoire: "Let Your Body Learn," "Murderous," and "Join in the Chant." Familiar from the dance clubs I had frequented.

Not only was I exhilarated by the performance of Nitzer Ebb, but I came to appreciate something about the nature of entertainment and, by extension, art. On the face of it, McCarthy's manically repeating brutal lyrics over mechanically thumping rhythms should be perceived as intimidating, or at least depressing. Instead, like so much of art and entertainment that deals with anger, horror, and the like, it has a positive, invigorating effect. Painters Francis Bacon and Lucien Freud; moviemakers Tim Burton, Wes Craven, and Brian De Palma; writers Edgar Allen Poe, H. P. Lovecraft, and Mary Shelley—all create art that jars our senses and, by extension, our emotions in a variety of ways. Industrial music, done right, strips away all the trappings of conventional entertainment featuring violence, suspense, and repulsion and gets right down to evoking those elemental emotional responses.

Jane's Addiction at Wellmont in Montclair

In March of 2010, Jane's Addiction performed at the Wellmont Theater in Montclair. I considered attendance mandatory, so I got us so-called VIP tickets, which proved a bust, since they didn't confer rights to any advantaged viewing spots.

Perry Farrell lived up to his reputation, forged in the annual Lolapalooza festivals of which he was the mastermind, for grand extravaganza on stage. I could hardly take in the spectacle featuring the prodigious repertoire and magnificent performance of Jane's Addiction—then the mother ship of all things alternative in the world of postpunk music—in front of a backdrop of giant nude statues, disorienting vintage film footage, and fetish-clad dancer/contortionists.

I was overtaken with the delusion that Dave Navarro's two-and-a-half-minute virtuoso guitar solo during the song "Three Days" represented an achievement that belonged in a category with my favorite piece of music, Beethoven's forty-minute Piano Concerto No. 5. Witnessing it live was one of several transcendent aesthetic experiences from which I have never fully recovered. The delusion persists in my mind to this day.

Skinny Puppy Valentine

Valentine's Day in 2014 provided a very special experience for lovers of industrial music. The object of their love, Skinny Puppy, fulfilled the wishes of a sellout crowd at NYC's Webster Hall. It was the Countess's and my special holiday experience.

It began with the obscure and rhythmless strains of the track "Choralone" from the *Rabies* album. The stage became lit, and Nivek Ogre came on wearing the first of several horrific costumes he would don throughout the show. The music transitioned seamlessly into the song "IllisiT" in which Skinny Puppy repeatedly accuses *this* of being "the criminal age."

The stage and Ogre were flooded with a crazy quilt of broken animated lighting, not exactly stroboscopic, but with a similar fragmenting effect that was disorienting and hallucinatory. As the band went through a wide variety of their recent works, an onstage screen ran LED figures displaying the rapidly growing national debt, at that time $55 trillion and rapidly mounting. Other screens displayed electronic circuit boards, disaster footage, chaos, and Op Art. Soon enough they went into their classic repertoire, culminating with our all-time favorite, "Warlock," the uniquely cadenced, mesmerizing hit from the *Rabies* album. As they continued alternating between the older and newer material, Ogre simulated cutting himself with a large dagger, then donned a hideous expressionless mask and hood, vaguely resembling the nightmarish figure of Death from Ingemar Bergman's *The Seventh Seal.* They performed another song, then bid "Thank you, New York," before taking a brief break, only to return with "Smothered Hope" and "Far Too Frail" before concluding with a track from their most recent album, *Weapon* (2013).

Throughout the show Ogre had worn now a furry costume, then a hazmat suit, a terrifying headdress or two, and had poured himself—and drank—a tall glass of a repulsive phosphorescent blue-green liquid. All we could think was how generous Skinny Puppy was in their unbounded efforts to please, shock, and entertain their zealous and loving fans, making that a Valentine's Day to remember.

Combichrist and Explicit Lyrics

Back in 1984, Tipper Gore, then-wife of then-senator Al Gore started a movement to, if not censor, at least label records and music for "explicit" lyrics. She was awakened to the issue by listening to her eleven-year-old daughter's copy of Prince's *Purple Rain* album. Much of the music that we were exposed to in the Goth, and especially industrial, scene would fall into that category; but none more so than a show we attended in 2014 at the Theater of the Living Arts in Philadelphia featuring aggrotech/industrial metal band Combichrist.

Following the opening, very explicit act by controversial and bizarre solo performer, William Control, the room went dark and the members of Combichrist took their places on stage while a militaristic orchestral fanfare filled the air. A robotic British-accented recorded voice announced, "We love you...now die." Wearing a hideous red mask, Norwegian lead vocalist, Andy LaPlegua, burst onstage screaming, "Hate, disorder, love, destroy," and the crowd joined in, chanting that venomous mantra.

Inevitably, a mosh pit formed of uninhibited punk rock girls to sounds of "Today I Woke To the Rain of Blood," "Throat Full of Glass," and the decidedly explicit "What the Fcuk Is Wrong with You?" The set closed with "Love Is a Razorblade." But the audience demanded more, so Combichrist came back on stage to sing "Fcuk that S—t" and "Sent to Destroy."

Tipper Gore's Parents Music Resource Center can perhaps take credit for Combichrist's reversing the *u* and the *c* in the famous F-word, sanitizing the obscenity by so doing.

COVER BANDS OR TRIBUTE BANDS

Cover bands are a big phenomenon in the Goth scene. Not that there aren't a great number of newer, original bands that came along in the '90s and the 2000s with a Goth or postpunk sound, but the reality is that most of the classic bands arose and flourished in the late 1970s and early '80s. Very few of these revered punk-era founders survive into the present. But for those who wish for a live performance experience simulating The Clash, The Ramones, or Joy Division, there are cover bands.

Since the great, classic postpunk bands were by and large gone or went away during the era of the '90s and the 2000s, with notable exceptions, many amateur and garage bands sought to recreate the live experience for fans by learning to perform the repertoires of defunct favorite groups. One NJ musician stood out by virtue of his versatility and sheer energy as well as his ability to organize band members to engage with him in various projects.

Fred Zoeller is a singer/guitarist with a wide, almost encyclopedic repertoire of rock music. He is a high-ranking Goth for his participation in numerous local and regional Goth bands, most notably the Empire Hideous and Five Star Dive. Fred's talents are so superior that he can sound like a lead professional vocalist and at the same time can handle almost any complicated and unique guitar playing.

Fred became enamored of alternative music when he was a freshman in high school under the influence of an older classmate. His friend's credentials included being a "rad skateboarder and competitive cyclist with badass Oakley sunglasses, a Swatch watch and a music collection that changed my life," says Fred. He mentions the good fortune of sufficient proximity to Long Island-based radio station 92.7 WLIR. That's where he furthered his interest in bands like the Smiths, Depeche Mode, the Cure, Erasure, New Order, and the like.

Recalling a turning point in his career, Fred tells the following:

> I played guitar in a few bands but it wasn't until I met another musician, David Sempier through an ad where we were both looking for a situation to form an original band that sounded like the Cure... We went on to form a band called Untitled Art and then changed the name to Five Star Dive. We played many gigs locally throughout NJ/NYC. But it was many lineup changes that challenged us. Many times we would play gigs as a duo and sample the drums, keys and

> bass just to avoid having to work with other musicians that weren't as engaged as us.
>
> Which led to the night in 2005 when we opened up for a friend's band The Empire Hideous at CBGBs in NYC. After that show, David spoke to Myke Hideous and said how we were having trouble keeping a regular line up and Myke was also looking for a new guitar and bass player. So David said we're putting our band on hold and we're joining the Empire Hideous. I was floored. I had seen them play and knew it was a much more professional situation to be involved in. I became very close with Myke and have stayed in the band still until this day. I have been fortunate to travel and play venues as far away as California and Canada.

Fred's taste in music runs from the immensely popular post-punk icons the Smiths, the Cure, Depeche Mode, Joy Division, and New Order. He doesn't shun well-known mainstream or "alternative" bands U2, Placebo, R.E.M., or The Killers. For darkwave Goth, Fred favors Bella Morte.

Modern English and Disorder

One night, in 2013, we were invited by the members of the Joy Division tribute band, Disorder, to a show at a venerable Jersey Shore dive-bar/nightclub The Saint in Asbury Park. Besides maintaining Christmas lights on the interior walls year-round, the venue was notable for a spacious, elevated stage, and a superb sound system.

Headlining the show was a new-wave-era Brit punk band Modern English. Like many outstanding groups from that period, they were from England and had enjoyed promotion by DJ John Peel who hosted them for a couple of sessions on his BBC radio show. They got an early start with 4AD Records. Modern English were famous for their megahit "I Melt with You," one of the most beloved songs of a generation. Despite numerous breakups and reunions, they represented the full original band except for the drummer, who appeared to be half the age of the others of the group. They performed exceedingly well and drew thunderous applause when they sang "I Melt with You."

But we were primarily interested in our friend, drummer Chris Mele's cover band who had chosen to reprise the repertoire of the foundational, iconic band Joy Division.

For the band Disorder's opening number, they began with fast-paced "Shadowplay," one of Joy Division's dark entries in a notably dark body of work. They then proceeded to "Disorder," the emotionally charged repetitious piece after which the band takes its name. Through the rest of the set it became apparent that this band had succeeded in capturing every musical nuance of the original's morose "She's Lost Control," "Atmosphere," and the haunting "Dead Souls."

A playbill featuring Modern English and the reincarnated Joy Division tribute band Disorder proved to be an interesting pairing. Joy Division is an iconic band, one of the cornerstone founders of Goth rock but produced a mere two studio albums. They went out of existence in only two years and hasn't more than a handful of recognizable hits. Modern English, by contrast, has a relatively vast body of work including seven studio albums spanning 1980–2010 and performs a wide spectrum of new and old classic songs. "I Melt with You," their one crucial hit is probably essential to more record collections, iTunes libraries, and MP3 downloads than everything by Joy Division combined.

We would find ourselves attending performances of the tribute band Disorder again and again in the future, trying to capture and understand the significance of Joy Division and the pivotal role it plays in founding the Goth subculture. Listening to their live, faithful interpretations seemed to serve that purpose better than looking at the originals on grainy archival video footage with poor sound quality.

Britain vs. the Bowery

One night in 2015 the aforementioned Saint in Asbury Park hosted three cover bands representing three distinct styles associated with the punk era. The night was called "Britain vs. the Bowery."

Rockaway Bitches, fronted by an imposing female, groomed and costumed to resemble Joey Ramone (disheveled hair, eyeglasses, and motorcycle jacket), recreated the New York Punk originals with twenty short songs including "Blitzkried Bop," "KKK," "Sedated," "Rock 'n' Roll Highschool," and "Rockaway Beach," from which the band took its double-entendre name. Just like the Ramones, they opened each number with the signature shout of "One, two, three, four!" the original band's way of emphasizing the do-it-yourself punk style of music.

Next up, Straight to Hell, a finely tuned Clash cover band, came on, capturing the subversive style of the original with eighteen songs that included "London's Calling," "I Fought the Law," "Should I Stay," and "Death or Glory."

Disorder once again masterfully revived British postpunk band Joy Division, starting with "Warsaw," a selection from the band's debut EP, *An Ideal for Living.* Disorder proceeded to meticulously recreate most of the Joy Division favorites: "Day of the Lords," "She's

Lost Control," "Isolation," "Dead Souls," and more. True to the dark, brooding *oeuvre* of the originals, they ended with the most somber of entries in the Joy Division body of work: "Ceremony" and "Twenty-Four Hours."

We came away with the inescapable conclusion embodied by the battle cry: punk never dies!

THE AFTERLIFE OF PUNK: AN INTERVIEW WITH MIKE NESS

Social Distortion started in the late 1970s as a hard-core California punk band inspired by the Sex Pistols. In the early 1980s, its lead singer, Mike Ness fell into drug addiction, from which neither he nor the band recovered until 1986. From that time forward, the style took on elements of country and western, honky-tonk, and "cow-punk." By the time of my 2008 *Aquarian*-commissioned interview with him, he was touring as the Mike Ness solo act. He made clear however that Social Distrotion was going to continue to perform and record in the future, as indeed it has.

He admitted that much of the darkness in his earlier works as Social D had been a reflection of negative experiences he was going through at the time. His later emergence as a cultural icon and the overcoming of past issues had brought him to a sense of gratitude for not only having survived as a popular performer, but for the increasing acclaim that seemed to grow with every passing year and every musical project he undertook. And this was manifest in his increasing focus on what he called roots music—the honest, folksy, and traditional voice of the people, as filtered through him, a punk icon, in essence, "cowpunk."

The summer stage at Asbury Park's Stone Pony afforded us an opportunity to pay homage to the punk roots of our scene when we attended a performance of not Social Distortion, but of Mike Ness, now a punk-influenced country and rock band. Regardless of category, a slam-dancing mosh pit formed the moment Mike Ness began to sing. Behind him was a huge poster with cartoonishly drawn images suggesting 1940s cinema noir: a fedora-hatted, Tommy gun wielding G-man kicking in a door, a lingerie-clad B-girl, strewn liquor bottles, and high-heel shoes.

Amid a song list with titles alluding to a remorse-worthy existence—"Don't Drag Me Down," "Alone and Forsaken," "Far Behind"—there were covers including the Stones' "Wild Horses" and June Carter's "Ring of Fire."

Our hearts were touched when Ness spoke to the crowd of his deep sense of admiration and indebtedness to the "roots music," of Hank Williams and other traditional folk and country-and-Western artists that had inspired him. To top it, he spotted a half dozen kids in the audience and called them up onstage and admonished them to apply themselves at school as best they could for their future benefit. Some punk!

Mike Ness oil on canvas (2018)

PERSONALITIES OF THE SCENE

Several individuals of importance to the Goth scene have been mentioned earlier in the book. The following section turns the focus upon certain specific participants and creators of the scene, not just because their role and contribution to the subculture has been monumental but because their stories are exemplary. Their personal histories as well as those of individuals profiled earlier in the book are representative of a broad sampling of scenesters and without fostering stereotypes or clichés. Each comes to the world of Goth through uniquely individual pathways but at the same time share recognizably similar origins.

Aurelio Voltaire

Aurelio Voltaire, as noted, was emcee at the 2004 Goth Award Ceremony. He was previously known by just the monomer "Voltaire" and is a towering figure in the NYC Goth scene recognized as multitalented and successful at many projects, roles, and functions that intersect with and support this subculture. He began his career in his teen years creating stop-motion advertisement videos for big name products like Budweiser, IKEA, Marvel, and many others. He created award-winning station IDs for SyFy Channel and MTV, one of which, "MTV Bosch," was based on the fifteenth-century-artist Hieronymus Bosch's "Garden of Earthly Delights," and was included in the famous time capsule of twentieth-century programming that was sent into space. In addition, he creates dark-themed toys, books, and comics and makes film shorts with famous stars of the alternative music scene.

Most fans of the Goth music scene know Aurelio Voltaire from his dark cabaret performances and recordings. He has about a dozen albums and keeps producing them about an album a year, often in collaboration with Goth rock stars in their own right. Voltaire's stage performance showcases his song writing, singing, stand-up comedy, and storytelling accompanied by European flavored guitar and fiddle music. His sarcastic lyrics put his music into the category of antifolk, wherein traditional sentiment is turned on its head and corny softheartedness is gleefully skewered.

Both in song and during asides between songs, he usually issues good-natured insults at the spectators. "Your tears are all the pay I'll ever need," he sings half-seriously, drawing roars of laughter rather than protest from his audience. He saves his strongest criticism and meanest jokes for New Jersey, where he reports having had unpleasant experiences during his early years growing up. Perhaps his persona, a mix of arrogance and self-deprecation, enables him to get away with such snide humor. Aurelio Voltaire can even elicit enthusiastic approval from the crowd of Goths when his mocks the pretensions that underlie the very subculture with the lyrics of his anthem, "The Vampire Club."

One of many occasions to attend a live performance by Aurelio Voltaire took place in 2002 at the club night called *Albion at Downtime* in midtown Manhattan. Not unexpectedly, accompanied by a violinist and himself on guitar, he opened with a parody of a Rammstein number, taking down that revered and all-too-seriously Germanic iconic band a notch or two. The rest of his set consisted of several songs in the aforementioned antifolk, minor key mode, sounding like Eastern European, Russian, or even Middle Eastern melodies. His monologue consisted of a "roast" all things Goth, targeting himself, his adoring fans in the audience, and religion. An original piece titled "The Man Upstairs" might have been about a neighbor on the floor above or might have been metaphorical blasphemy. A tango-paced number, "When You're Evil," served as a sly autobiographical confession of his own less-than-admirable glee at the misfortunes of others.

Aurelio Voltaire brought this stage persona to the Wave Gotik Treffen in 2016 on stage at the Heathen Village, where he put on a captivating, jolly, and mildly offensive skit, poking fun at both his German hosts and his fellow New Yorkers that had come to attend his show. As the opening or headline entertainer at events like the Steampunk World's Fair, he often serves as master of ceremonies. A good example was the 2004 Goth Awards at CBGB's Gallery, where he performed "Vampire Club," his hilarious spoof of those who role-play at being vampires, which then turned into an impromptu stand-up comedy act, making sarcastic comments while handing out certificates and awards. Spectators and recipients alike were giddy with laughter, even at themselves.

Besides meeting the worldwide demand for Aurelio Voltaire to appear, perform, and emcee international Goth events, he has continued to produce creative video projects. He maintains a prolific YouTube channel that includes numerous and ongoing full seasons of his Gothic homemaking show and monthly, interactive "Nooseletters" in which he keeps his fans and followers aware of his current projects and scheduled live performances.

Andi Harriman

How does a girl who grew up in the Appalachian Mountains of Southwest Virginia grow up to be one of, if not *the*, leading authority on the subculture called Goth?

An interview of Ms. Harriman provided us some answers and took us on a journey tour of the entire Goth-industrial music world.

She reports that where she grew up there was no postpunk/Goth scene. Yet there were lots of mall kids who loved NIN, Tool, and Marilyn Manson. Initially, that sort of aggressive music wasn't her thing at the time nor did the clothes appeal to her. By chance, at age fifteen, she encountered the Cure's "Just like Heaven" video. She loved how feminine Robert Smith looked, what with his lipstick applied so sloppily across his face and his backcombed hair. It was poppy enough to feel familiar to her since she had grown up on easy listening radio: Phil Collins, Journey, and synth songs. However, there was a sadness to "Just like Heaven" that appealed to her adolescent, melancholic, perspective, which was to become her self-described and persistent outlook on life.

She bought the Cure's *Kiss Me, Kiss Me, Kiss Me* (1987) at the used CD store and also happened to pick up Depeche Mode's *Music for the Masses* CD soon after. She views these two CDs as the gateway to her Goth destiny. At the time, she definitely didn't realize there was an entire subculture around darker music, having grown up in a town of eight thousand people and finding it difficult to know much beyond her limited personal experience and what was shown on TV. As time went on, her youth came to be devoted to the musical decade of the eighties, based largely on esoteric recordings culled from the thrift store.

She went on for many years not knowing about a Goth scene despite her love for darker/alternative eighties music. The late-night TV program *VH1 Classic* became her favorite thing to watch in the mid-2000s. Peter Murphy; The Church; Depeche Mode; and feminine, androgynous folks who sang about the darker sides of life captivated her.

In the late 2000s, she fed off beautiful photos of Goths on Tumblr. She befriended and eventually collaborated with Marloes Bontjie, then a blogger and creator of the defunct but archived "Now This Is Gothic!" Tumblr. He would later collaborate on her book *Some Wear Leather Some Wear Lace: The Worldwide Compendium of Postpunk and Goth in the 1980s.*

In 2010, she moved from Virginia to Savannah, Georgia, a town dominated by its famous art college, and went to her first Goth party in the summer of 2011. During an internship in New York City, she attended the Red Party on a night featuring the music of the Sisters of Mercy. The following year, 2012, she took the eighteen-hour Amtrak ride and moved to NYC with arrangement to sleep on a friend's couch until getting settled. At the time, she was heavily involved with trying to find a publisher for her book, eventually arranging publication with Intellect Books.

Andi began regularly attending the Depeche Mode Fan Club in NYC among other recurring parties (e.g., the short-lived venture called Discipline, Arkham, and the longevity champ Defcon and such venues as the Acheron, Don Pedro's in Brooklyn, and the venerable Pyramid through 2013). She saw those events as her home and the world in which she feels that she has found community.

She had her first taste of the European scene when she attended the Wave Gotik Treffen, exhilarated by the ways in which it differed from that with which she was familiar in the States.

Andi got her first gig deejaying in late 2013 at Arkham at Don Pedro, under the auspices of veteran DJ Jose Frances. Soon after, in September of 2014, her book, *Some Wear Leather*...was published, thereafter packing her calendar with signings and release events, as far away as Berlin, and began being treated as Goth royalty.

That year she founded her own event, Synthicide, at which to serve as DJ, first as a Sunday happy hour at the Bossa Nova Civic Club, subsequently as a Thursday night party. She has also hosted live band performances at two other Brooklyn venues, Brooklyn Bazaar and St. Vitus.

Kai and The Sedona Effect

In 2014, we attended a screening of a striking music video by The Sedona Effect, a dark electro band fronted by classically trained soprano and dramatist Kai Irina Hahn. The video featured mesmerizing, layered electro-industrial tracks, and several crescendos. While onscreen, Kai took the form of a femme fatale, bathed alternately in eerie blue and red light. A large, slithering, spotted python weaved its way through the video and around Kai's persona.

After the video, Kai put on a live action performance of "Gloomy Sunday."

Kai Irina Hahn

Known around NYC perhaps best for The Sedona Effect, her distinctly original EBM/industrial project, Kai has been described as "Nina Hagen meets Billy Holiday." She traces her life in music back to early childhood and a self-taught pianist father. Music played constantly in the home. Memories of family life included regular gatherings around the piano, singing everything from Mozart to Broadway hits.

Although Kai never took piano lessons, she learned enough by herself to begin composing original songs on its black-and-white keyboard. She took formal studies on violin and viola throughout high school and transposed her piano compositions to be played on these string instruments. But she was even more drawn to theater where dance and her music came together.

Around age fifteen, Kai joined forces with a young poet to create a dark folk/darkwave band that drew upon her interests in Gothic themes and mythology. Within two years, her music was being promoted on a compilation by a Bavarian Goth zine called *Astan*, which exposed her to professional studio production. A world-changing experience at the Wave Gotik Treffen in 1998 led Kai to remain for three years in Leipzig studying theater. She continued those studies in Berlin and Paris before applying her theatrical efforts in a large-scale circus that toured Europe for two seasons. After this, she moved to London and continued taking lessons in singing and dance.

Her next move was to NYC and the metropolitan Goth scene where Kai felt enthralled by the city, its people, and its multifaceted and inexhaustible energy. She shifted from classical music to electronic. Together with a collaborator named Preston Krafft, she started writing songs, including "Cross the Line," which became the foundation of The Sedona Effect, her fluid, rotating band of performers.

Kai went out dancing almost every other night, and during one of her frequent nights out, she met with Goth-industrial celebrity Athan Maroulis. They shared a common interest in the culture and music of the 1920s. After a second chance encounter at the Triton Festival, Maroulis invited Kai to join his new band project, NØIR, and she agreed to sign on as keyboardist and backup vocalist. He also introduced her to Xris Smack, who recorded and produced a series of Sedona Effect originals at Mindswerve Studios.

One of Kai's major projects and proudest achievements, the video for the song "Cross the Line," drew participation from numerous talented individuals as well as a baby boa constrictor named Loki and was shot during one of the last Redrum Balls at the now defunct R Bar. More and more, she was fusing her several passions for composition, dance, songwriting, and theatrics. Kai's shows might mingle live performances with film presentations, music videos, and interactive theater. One of the most noteworthy and successful of these was the Annual Gothic Vampire Cruise.

For the four years in a row preceding the pandemic lockdown, her unique and popular project, the Gothic Vampire Cruise, shipped out on a 150-feet schooner from NY harbor for hours long of dark-themed entertainment and theatrics involving actors and the appropriately costumed audience of passengers.

Kai confesses that as a child she was frightened of witches. Yet she was drawn to the dark side by what she calls "the prospect of a hidden, mysterious secret to be unraveled by putting aside the customary fear of death." At age five she was glued to the TV for a program called *Wunschfilm*, where she tried to influence the broadcasting of Dracula films by phone-in voting under her mother's supervision. By high school, she was penning papers about vampires in cinema and literature.

Kai also identifies with the nonconformity, imagination, and creativity that are associated with a passion for all things Gothic. She sees the NYC Goth scene as one where rebellion against the norm, extravagant lifestyle and acceptance of eccentricity are celebrated.

Kai's favorites include classic industrial bands Einstürze Neubauten and VNV Nation and Assemblage 23; postpunk Goth groups such as the Cure, Bauhaus, Peter Murphy, Depeche Mode, Nick Cave, Siouxsie, Gary Numan, Wolfsheim, and Diary of Dreams; and German bands Deine Lakaien and Silke Bischoff (the obscure band named after a notorious 1988 kidnapping case).

Madame X

Few can claim as broad and as deep commitment to the Goth scene as Madame X. Like many other scenesters, she has chosen a moniker to place some distance between her day-to-day life and what she calls her nightside involvement, playing off her actual surname, Xavier.

Born and raised in what was then fascist Portugal, she was sheltered from music, cinema, and fashions related to Gothic influences; yet she imbibed something of the dark aesthetic of Portugal's pervasively Catholic culture with its embrace of dark rituals and eerie celebrations. Black mourning attire was widely seen, but she was prohibited from indulging her childhood wish to be dressed in black. When the regime changed, she quickly and avidly sought out books and cinema with occult and macabre topics. After moving to the US, she accessed information about comparative religions, shamanism, Eastern philosophies, and metaphysics.

Her ethnic roots pointed her in the direction of visiting convents, teaching Sunday school, and considering becoming a nun. Her inner directive however was toward a more profound, multifaceted, spirituality—a spirituality that was universal. She found herself attracted to gnosticism, paganism, and a frequent attendee at *botanica*-sponsored gatherings and rituals. She befriended a witch queen and hung out with journalist Tony Sokol of Vampyre Theater fame and with fetish photographer Nighthawk Scarpa.

At the same time, she began immersing herself in the punk scene and its music. She shopped at Café Soundz, Black on Black, and Romp & Stomp in Montclair, New Jersey, for music and outfits. A UHF channel that was the precursor to MTV exposed her to Devo, the Plasmatics, Adam Ant, Blondie, and The Damned. Proximity of her New Jersey digs to NYC facilitated trips to see Agnostic Front and Suicidal Tendencies at the Ritz.

Attending the NY Renaissance Faire in the early nineties, she was stunned by beautifully clad Goths. She followed them to clubs including Aldo's and the Pipeline, where she saw Nine Inch Nails and the Empire Hideous. She was to go on to develop friendships with Emilio and many other club owners and promoters. She attended what she calls special vampire gatherings at various clubs including the Cat Club, The Mission, and Le Bar Bat. Madame X was a regular at the Bank, Coney Island High, Mother's, especially at those nights designated Long Black Veil and Contempt. At the Limelight and Webster Hall, she took in countless world-famous acts and obscure, offbeat performances as well as special events.

Creating the Rift Arts Forum Publication for original art, poetry, and short stories led her to staging events; open-mikes; and gatherings at cafes, galleries, nightclubs and even on cable TV.

Madame X is one of the most widely traveled persons in the Goth scene as she continued to broaden her spiritual outlook by trips to the pyramids and mystical remains of ancient Mexico. In London, she attended the Slimelight as well as toured what she calls haunted sites like the Tower of London, Stonehenge, and Canterbury. In the Netherlands, she explored the local art, culture, and Goth scene and ended up ascending to the status of high priestess of a mystical order. She discovered and lived the Goth scene in Sao Paulo and frequented music venues like Madame Satan.

In 2007, she explored First Nation citadels, petroglyphs, and sacred grounds in Nevada, Arizona, and Colorado. She sipped absinthe at a desert ceremony in Idaho and explored the ancient culture and exotic landscapes of Oahu, Hawaii. She spent time in Ireland studying fabled sites, abbeys, and cemeteries.

Madame X's travels introduced her to Taino culture in Puerto Rico, to the catacombs and nightlife in Paris, and to the haunts of Romania, whence she returned with Transylvanian soil for special friends. Domestically, she has traveled the major cities of the US and Canada in order to attend Convergence gatherings and to explore each town and its cemeteries, churches, and haunted locations. Goth Cons 2000 and 2001 brought her to the south, Atlanta, and New Orleans, specifically.

Thereafter, she moved to Savannah, a town dominated by an extensive art college, where she was to reside for five years. Sensing that the Goth scene needed recharging, she initiated the Savannah Goth Survey; headed the GA chapter of Bloodlines International; hosted Goth, art, and fetish events; and collaborated in the formation of Club Illuminati to produce parties, Gothabilly-themed events, and live performance presentations.

Back in NYC, she regularly attended Alchemy and other events at CBGB's Gallery and sometime served as hostess or announcer for special acts. And in Newark (in 1998, 1999, and 2000), Madame X and a male cohort (twice Lord Vahmp and once Myke Hideous) hosted the NJ Goth Challenge at which a panel of respected judges from the scene evaluated candidates to be dubbed "Mistress" and "Master" of the statewide Goth scene. She was also attended high-level gatherings as a member of corporate Goth that sponsored dinners, museum visits, club outings, and movie nights. She founded her own coven, the House of Dreaming, for pagans of all stripes.

Madame X has contributed abundantly to books and publications like *Gothic Beauty Magazine*, *Vampyre Almanac*, *The Sanguinomicon*, and *The Goth Bible*. She was frequently featured on the late nineties cable program *Vampyre Lounge* as interviewer. She has cohosted the Gothic Vampire Cruise and has appeared in the Empire Hideous music video "Pretty Faces."

In 2015, Madame X established the Iron Garden, an organization that meets regularly at QXT's to serve as "a Safe Haven for NJ Nightkind." Over the years, IG has featured authors, teachers, visual artists, psychic readers, ritual leaders, performance artists, and bands like the Long Losts and Baron Misuraca.

Her schedule of special activities was suspended during the Covid pandemic but has sprung back energetically in its aftermath.

Athan Maroulis

Vocalist Athan Maroulis has collaborated with Kai and her fellow keyboardist Demetra Songs to form a band, NØIR, that combines many of the musical and cultural background influences that he brings to the stage and recording studio. His story encapsulates the rise of a fan to a star of the Goth-industrial music scene. He traces his entry into the scene in 1986 and lists his favorite postpunk/Goth bands as Psychedelic Furs, Japan, Bauhaus, Siouxsie and the Banshees, and the Sisters of Mercy. His favorite industrial bands are Fad Gadget, Ministry, Leaether Strip, Killing Joke, and Cabaret Voltaire.

He recalls the term *Goth* was just starting to be used to describe what had previously been called alternative or underground music. Some were using the term *postpunk*, or Batcave, and, on the West Coast, *deathrock*. Athan remembers the smoky, dimly lit clubs like Danceteria in Manhattan where one might hear Sisters of Mercy or Siouxsie and the Banshees in a mix that was considered "late new wave." Included in that stew were New Order, Depeche Mode, Fad Gadget, Visage, Yaz, and the Smiths.

As a real-life experience, it resembled the opening scene of the movie *The Hunger* (1983). He was struck by the collision of two icons of the scene, which he described as "Bowie meets Bauhaus." Athan saw that movie as launching him into a new lifestyle, a new aesthetic, in which the real-world mimicked cinema art, which mimicked his real-life experience.

Yet by the time of Athan's awakening to this new world, Bauhaus had broken up, and Ian Curtis had passed away, leaving him a collection of Joy Division albums but seemingly no future material. That pessimism was to dissolve away when, in the mideighties, Athan dropped acid and went out record shopping. Rummaging through bins in a West Village record store, he stumbled upon a newly imported album by the Sisters of Mercy. He was pleased to have discovered an active band that he could follow. That summer he saw the Sisters of Mercy live at the Ritz, standing on tiptoe to enhance his already-considerable height, in order to glimpse the tops of their Amish-style hats beyond the swarming crowd. Amid the darkness, the drama, the glamour, and the Vampira-resembling girls, Athan felt he had found his "thing." It meshed well with his interest in Bronte, Poe, and dark literature and poetry.

Soon, capitalizing on his vocal talents, and over the years since then, Athan came to sing lead for such varied dark music bands as Spahn Ranch, Fahrenheit 451, Executive Slacks, Black Tape for a Blue Girl, and now NØIR.

Presently, Athan also serves as director of publicity for Metropolis Records, the Philadelphia-based label that showcases electronic and darkwave artists to the world.

Xris SMack and Stimulate

Ashley Bad and Xris SMack! with conventioneer

We developed a special relationship with impresario Xris SMack and attended many of his events. He serves as DJ, engineer, and promoter of New York-based, fetish-themed musical parties since 1996, namely, the biannual SMack! And he established Stimulate as, the premier, recurring dance-night version in 2008.

These events of late often took place at Drom, a nightclub and performance space on Avenue A in the East Village, although by no means exclusively in that location. Xris and a handful of carefully chosen DJs curate a sophisticated and encyclopedic spectrum of Goth, darkwave, punk, postpunk, and eccentric rarities to which the crowds of savvy attendees dance while attractive and fetish-attired performers cavort on a stage overlooking the dance floor.

Gothic-industrial musical acts from the region as well as superstar bands from around the world typically come on stage late in the evenings and showcase their repertoire, often spiced with creative acts of performance art.

The crowd of attendees inevitably included the glitterati and celebrities of the NYC and regional Goth-industrial-postpunk scene.

The center of attention was invariably his protégé at the time of our attendance, the Latex Lady of Stimulate, Ashley Bad. Ms. Bad has relocated to the West Coast, but her story is an important facet of the NYC Goth-industrial culture.

Ashley Bad and Fetish in the Goth Scene

Punk couture has included fetish attire from London sex shops since its very inception, as a form of defiance and intentional offensiveness. The attachment that most Goths have to the color black made for a natural acceptance, even approval, of the predominantly black adornments of fetish. Like many other things, it took on a life of its own as the inherent appeal of black leather and skintight rubber outfits resonated with the alternative lifestyles of many artists, models, musicians, and other inhabitants of this particular demimonde. It also serves as a way of amplifying the intrinsically libertine and ultratolerant attitude toward sexual matters and diversity within the Goth scene. A foremost representative of this particular facet or tributary of Goth is statuesque, latex-wearing model and dancer Ashley Bad. For the better part of a decade, ending in 2020, she had been a functioning hostess at these events, a lively sort of center of attention, often surrounded by the proverbial "bevy of beauties" who served as her entourage, going about extending friendly greetings among attendees and graciously posing for photos.

Ashley began her involvement in the NYC underground scene when her stunning physical attributes resulted in her recruitment to model at a mini fetish event in Chinatown when she was still in college and below drinking age. At the same time, she already carried with her an obsessive taste for Goth rock, dark wave, metal, industrial, and all its hybrids. She cultivated her taste for this kind of music with Napster downloads during her teen years, fed by the contrasting experience of attending Catholic high school.

Ashley came to idolize pinup and glamour models like Bettie Page and Rita Hayworth, finally coming to admire and emulate the modern latex vixens Dita von Teese and Rubberdoll. Her early dating experiences attending clubs in NYC led her to acquaintance and involvement with nightlife performers and underground artists. Xris SMack made Ashley an integral part of his long-running SMack! event and the then-newly established series of parties dubbed Stimulate. At the same time, she was also working for latex fashion designers Latex Nemesis and Kirsten Li, performing as a model and crafting and designing latex outfits while helping to organize and promote events.

Ashley has performed with famous glam-punk shock rock band The Voluptuous Horror of Karen Black and headlined in diverse places like Montreal, Pittsburgh, and New Orleans, and at such events as the Bondage Ball, Fetish Marathon Ball, Last Rites Tattoo Theater, Darkside of the Con, and the Endless Night Vampire Ball. In 2019, she hosted her own event called She-Devil, a dark, fetishistic boudoir-style event featuring performing models with themes of Goth, camp, erotic feminism, kink, and LGBTQ+. Lately, she has been added to the lineup of the techno-industrial, "sextreme" performance band the Lords of Acid while she continues to work at designing devilish apparel, deejaying, and creating original music for livestreaming during the pandemic.

"Sir" William Welles

Sir William Welles was often a promoter and impresario in the NYC Goth scene. Since 2007, he had maintained a crucial website, New Goth City, with nationwide listings of underground club events, shopping for vintage clothing and accessories, Goth styles, dark-themed restaurants, bars and sightseeing recommendations.

In his late teen years, he identified as a "club kid," and by the late eighties, he was serving as a promoter of VIP parties at nightclubs such as the Limelight, Roxy, Pyramid, and the Tunnel. In addition, he developed an interest in horror films and skills in cinematic special effects, screenwriting, and directing and attended the School of Visual Arts to attain a BFA in film. He had to juggle his proclivity for movies and video with working in his family restaurant situated in the Hell's Kitchen of Manhattan.

Disappointed with his efforts at film, he found himself in a very dark place and fell into alcohol abuse, even suicidal thoughts. Somehow the darkness that had overtaken his soul facilitated his attraction for dark-themed art and aesthetics.

At the now defunct Tower Records store on Times Square, he spotted a copy of *Gothic Beauty* magazine and was immediately drawn to it. Everything in those pages spoke to him, likening his enthusiasm to that of a teenage boy with his first copy of *Playboy*. The darkness he had suffered under became his enlightenment, his source of joy, and a renewed identity.

He set about to find and enter the Goth scene wholeheartedly and started attending Cybertron Thursday nights at the Pyramid, Club Anubis, and Necromantic at the Knitting Factory. As his new identity blossomed, he drew comfort in the darkness, a shroud to embrace and signal his sadness and pain. He now inhabited his new identity, likened it to a closed, dimly lit room filled with moody music. He may have appeared to others as a creepy figure seated in a corner of the club, observing others; but he soon befriended the club promoters, DJs, bartenders, and bouncers.

During the years that followed, Sir William launched event after event including Labyrinth, with DJ Rob Station, and The Scarlet Parlour, a *salon noir* and performance event.

Whenever a holiday weekend cleared Monday for most workers, Sir William would arrange a club event termed The Redrum Ball on the preceding Sunday night. Thus the Countess and I would happily attend at the designated location on the Sunday night before Presidents' Day, MLK Day, Memorial Day, and Labor Day.

Always going for an extra edge, Welles typically announced a special theme each time. Sometimes it might be "Circus of Horrors" or "Demented Fairy Tales." One memorable occasion was themed "Rise of the Dark Side," blending such cinematic sci-fi icons as *Star Trek*, *Star Wars*, and *The Matrix*. Many, but not all, attendees attired themselves according one or the other leitmotif, wearing futuristic costumes. The rest wore always-acceptable, basic black. Besides star DJs Aengel and V-Christ, NJ's own Mindsolvent from QXT's took turns manning the turntables, maintaining a steady flow of the Cure, Peter Murphy, and Skinny Puppy.

As part of the entertainment, ecdysiast Cassandra Rosebeetle and another scantily clad actress enacted a silent, ballet-like pantomime of, what else, a murder.

Jeremy Bastard

Jeremy, whose real age was not revealed, and who describes himself as "emotionally, around sixteen," had no formal musical training but has always been what he describes as "a mega fan of music." His obsessive appreciation derived from listening to CDs, however, prepped him sufficiently that he was enabled to learn what he needed to play from picking the brains of musician friends. Still in his teen years, he accompanied older friends to Goth clubs on weekends where he became a regular attendee. When his roommate, who had started running a Goth club, ran into a problem, Jeremy, with his vast CD collection, stepped in. Inevitably, he moved into professional deejaying and was spinning with Mike Stalagmike at the Pyramid's Defcon on Saturdays and on Morrissey night at Paul's Casablanca in Soho before the pandemic.

Entering adulthood, he moved to NYC. Jeremy joined a short-lived "death-rock / mall punk" band, the Murdered. Members of that band went on to form groups like the Guiloteens, the Brickbats, and even work with Gitane De Mone, onetime member of Goth rock pioneers Christian Death. Entering adulthood, and moving to NYC, Jeremy joined the band Unto Ashes and eventually formed his own band, Autodrone. He learned music production by trial and error, partly from friends and partly from YouTube videos. He has found collaborating with musician associate to be somewhat problematic in the era of Covid social distancing.

Nowadays, Jeremy lists his all-time favorite post-punk/Goth bands as Joy Division, Sisters of Mercy, The Birthday Party, and the Stiffs. Skinny Puppy, Ministry Icon of Coil, and Mentallo, and the Fixer are as his top industrial bands.

WHAT I LEARNED ABOUT THE GOTH SUBCULTURE

The Goth aesthetic and ideology are properly identified with youth culture. Some may cast aspersions on the movement for fostering or espousing an immature, puerile mindset. Maturity and experience are the conventional values, certainly when it comes to rational planning. But childlike openness and suspension of disbelief serve the human psyche very well when it comes to life's enjoyments. There are wide variation in individual's openness to novel ideas and experiences. That openness, so closely associated with youth and adolescence, is usually present in large measure among Goths who tend to hold on to this outlook well into their later lives.

The Goth mindset, values, and lifestyle are initially a reaction of the adolescent experience, which is foremost, one of disillusionment with realities of adulthood. This is a stage of life when the blissful naiveté of childhood confronts the cynicism-inducing realities of life, like eating the bitter fruit of the tree of knowledge. The reality and proximity of death are perceived for the first time. The illusions of fairy tales, simplistic explanations, and the hypocrisy of institutions like organized religion become recognized. Parents come to be seen for what they really are: fallible, frail, vulnerable, and mortal beings.

All of these revelations and disillusionments tend to promote a kind of rebelliousness, which can get channeled in myriad different ways. Goth is one way that is chosen, or perhaps imposed by the circumstances that prevail in the adolescent's world at the time of these insights. The dark aesthetic, the morbid preoccupations, the iconoclastic attitude, the defiant appearance, and the unconventional taste all follow from and are shaped by this cynical grasp. On the one hand, there is rejection of the values and conventions of mainstream (i.e., parental) society. On the other, there is mocking and exaggerated appropriation of such symbols as religious iconography; funeral attire; antiquated styles in fashion, music, and literature.

The Four Cornerstones

There are four main elements to Goth Subculture. They are intimately intertwined but can be parsed out as separate threads that are essential to the aesthetics of the scene.

The first is *music*. Goth music, or Goth rock as it sometimes is called, is an interlinked offshoot of the postpunk movement that starts with punk-rock, to which have been added electronic, Gothic, and industrial elements (each to be described below). It should be noted that all three of these tributaries are in the never-ending process of evolving. For example, during the 1990s punk gave rise to grunge, where the original brash, simplified, and antisocial musical style of punk survived in vestigial form. Likewise, the industrial music of the Cabaret Voltaire variety has given rise to the highly danceable EBM and all other kinds of commercially compatible, electronic, and synthetic styles.

Goth rock started as guitar-and-vocalist driven music but soon absorbed the electronic technology, especially *reverb*, available to either enhance or in some instances substitute for guitars and song in the conventional sense. What it hasn't lost is its generally morose and desperate quality. Its origins trace back to Bauhaus, Joy Division, the Cure, and Siouxsie and the Banshees. Melodies are usually minor key; lyrics often despairing; and the mood alarmed, plaintive, morose, or dissociative. Examples include "Bela Lugosi's Dead," "Dead Souls," and "Spellbound." Hugely popular bands like The Cure may have branched out into pop after establishing a body of work that was more conventionally Goth.

The next essential element is *fashion*. The Goth community originally adhered to a strict black wardrobe but has over the decades, since the eighties, come to incorporate the self-consciously retro-futuristic steampunk style with its Victorian and Edwardian look. Another sought-after and approved look is vampiric. Fetish attire has been borrowed. Its original incorporation in the London punk scene; and formal attire, Egyptian, ceremonial, and postapocalyptic are all integrated into Goth fashion. Goth shuns denim, sneakers, fine footwear, business, and sports attire. Baseball caps and colorful cheerful patterns are never worn. Dyed-black hair is mainstream in the Goth scene; but unnatural, garish hair colors like green, purple, and magenta are standard, as are all variations of mohawk hairstyles, another element appropriated from the never-dying punk scene.

The third element is an intense commitment to *tolerance* of differences. In the interest of nonconformity, tolerance is quite universal in the Goth scene. The urge toward nonconformity often steers people into traps of utter conformity, but the Goth community avoids this by enforcing strict tolerance of variations in thought, dress, beliefs, philosophy, and lifestyle. Variations and lack of convention in sexual preference, gender identity, and personal style are all acceptable within the Goth community. Revolving around these core elements, the interests of Goths include gothic literature like that of Edgar Allan Poe or H. P. Lovecraft, classic horror movies from the early days of motion pictures, as well as modern makers of dark cinema like Tim Burton and David Lynch.

The fourth cornerstone of Goth culture is a fixation on *morbid preoccupations*: horror literature, cinema, folklore, and more. Many profess to having an affection for cemeteries, coffins, to symbols of skulls and skeletons, interest in autopsies, cadavers, cremation, burial rites, death-masks, and more. Some go so far as to make pets of domesticated spiders or tend to the veterinary care of bats, snakes, lizards, and other "repulsive" species associated with evil or aggression. Easily dismissed as offensive, morbid preoccupations permeate all our arts and sciences. Many are the scientists of varying disciplines who have a skull or a specimen jar on display on their desk. Stained-glass images in places of worship are filled with symbols of death and dying. Mozart, Brahms, and Verdi, among countless other classical composers, have each contributed a masterpiece requiem.

A survey of Goths on Facebook highlighted the list of their favorite filmmakers. Besides the litany of eighties and nineties slasher film artists (Wes Craven, Brian De Palma, John Carpenter, and Clive Barker), there remains an enduring esteem for the great, cinema artists like Tim Burton, Tod Browning (*Dracula*, *Freaks*), James Whale (*Frankenstein*, *The Invisible Man*), Val Lewton (I *Walked With a Zombie*, *Cat People*), Jan Svankmajer, the Brothers Quay, David Lynch, Guillermo Del Toro, and many others too numerous to list.

The Goth mentality is to develop a sort of friendly familiarity with the forces (human and otherwise) of evil, not in support of evil but rather to confront it without the usual fear. The attire, appearance, and preoccupations of Goth contain a significant element of self-conscious pretentiousness, or camp (the once-fashionable aesthetic style characterized by ostentatious and shocking excess).

Goth morality has little to do with organized religion. Instead, spiritual and philosophical interests run from Buddhism to pantheism to Wicca and beyond. Many Goths possess interests in higher culture, such as classical music, fine arts, and museum collections as long as they have a melancholy essence.

Politics has little role in the Goth world. Many Goths hold strong political views but rarely do they come to the fore. Unlike punk, from which Goth arises, there is little reference to politics except those peripheral issues like animal rights and vegetarianism. And even those issues do not succeed in dividing the community into opposing factions. There are, however, rare instances of ostracism of individuals who are outspoken activists in support of unpopular, usually conservative, ideology.

Goth does not support the kind of aggressive denunciation of society the way punk does, focusing instead on shared aesthetics, style, and taste. Thus, Goth has a vastly wider influence and presence in today's society than punk. So absent is true, original punk from the current world that its battle cry is "Punk is coming back!" There is no "back" from which Goth needs to come. The marginalization of political opinions has had a beneficial effect on the persistent survival of the Goth scene by avoiding conflict within the community so that the focus always remains on music, fashion, tolerance, and a dark aesthetic sense.

AFTERWORD

The year 2021 concluded thirty uninterrupted years devoted to these diverse but interrelated cultural phenomena. This book is the product of that experience.

Then Covid restrictions and lockdowns occurred. Clubs, museums, music halls—all shut down. There was seemingly endless delay in the reopening of Goth venues as well as eventual relocation of most of these to Brooklyn that I found I could no longer pursue the lifestyle in person. I had perhaps aged out of the scene.

As my writing for the *Aquarian* came to a gradual close, I began to put more effort into painting, my first love. I undertook to create a series of portraits of Goth Icons from the music scene and cinema. I began with Robert Smith of the Cure and Siouxsie Sioux of the Banshees. From there I launched into TV and cinema personalities like Bela Lugosi and Elvira. Eventually, such diverse icons as Wednesday Addams, Leonard Cohen, and Mary Woolstonecraft Shelley were committed to oil on canvas.

The Countess and I attended an exhibition of the photography of Myke Hideous in late 2013, marking five years since Myke had left music and the Goth scene. Photography, a family tradition, was a natural extension of his affinity for visual arts. Since 2008, Myke had devoted himself mainly to nature and photography, concentrating his efforts on landscapes, flora and fauna of his native New Jersey, and his new digs in rural Pennsylvania. On hiatus from the music world, he has returned with renewed focus on drawing, painting, sculpture, furniture and clothing design. Myke and The Empire Hideous (in semiretirement) under the duress of inspiration, make occasional music videos and rare live appearances for highly fortunate, exclusive audiences.

What happened to the Carmela whose stunning beauty and beguiling personality had triggered my thirty-year delving into the New Dark Age? I never did get to give her art lessons. Beyond all expectations and in defiance of the laws of time, space, and matter, she remains as beautiful as she was three decades ago. The girl, who modestly included a reference to "Fashion Faces" on her 1990-vintage business card, has gone on to boundless success as one of the most sought-after cosmetologists and become an internationally renowned makeup artist to the stars of television, advertising, and media.

As for the Countess, she moved with me to a semisecluded old house in a wooded area of New Jersey, where we try to keep our connection to the scene in an intermittent basis, making occasional appearance at QXT's and the Red Party, and always planning one more trip to Europe for another Castle Party or Wave Gotik Treffen.

Carmela Today

ABOUT THE AUTHOR

Doktor John is a retired orthopedic surgeon. For twenty years, he wrote regular reports on the Gothic, punk, and industrial scene for the *Aquarian*, a rock music magazine. He has previously published a novella, *San Rocco and the Egg Drop Soup*, about an identity crisis and enlightenment experienced during a European vacation.

CPSIA information can be obtained
at www.ICGtesting.com
Printed in the USA
LVHW021236240523
747874LV00003B/22